Muscle building: practical points for practical people

Gulick, Luther Halsey, 1865- [from old catalog]

SPALDING'S
ATHLETIC LIBRARY

PRICE 10 CENTS

MUSCLE
BUILDING

BY
LUTHER HALSEY GULICK M.D.

AMERICAN SPORTS PUBLISHING CO.
21 Warren Street, New York.

A. G. SPALDING & BROS.

Won a **Special Award** and a **Grand Prize**

for their Gymnasium Equipment at the World's Fair. The hundreds of Gymnasts who competed in the different events in the Stadium during the year proclaimed the apparatus made by A. G. Spalding & Bros. the best that they had ever worked on, and the team of German Turners that came to America especially to compete in the International Championships at St. Louis on July 1 and 2, 1904, requested that they be permitted to use the apparatus of the

Spalding Gymnasium Exhibit

in the Gymnastic Tournament, and at the conclusion of the two-day meeting, voluntarily forwarded to A. G. SPALDING & BROS. a testimonial highly complimenting the firm on the manufacture of their Gymnastic Apparatus. The same request was made by the Young Men's Christian Association of America, and the apparatus was used by them for the Championships with best results. In the International A.A.U. Championships A. G. Spalding & Bros.' apparatus was likewise used, and the Chairman of the Committee declared the apparatus to be the best ever used in connection with a championship meeting.

MUSCLE BUILDING

Practical Points

for

Practical People

LUTHER HALSEY GULICK, M. D.

President American Physical Education
Association—Director Physical Training Public Schools, New York City

Published by

AMERICAN SPORTS PUBLISHING CO.
15 Warren Street, New York City

COPYRIGHT, 1905

BY

AMERICAN SPORTS PUBLISHING COMPANY

NEW YORK

MUSCLE BUILDING

VIBRATORY EXERCISE.

Many business men at forty are fat and flabby; their arms are weak, their hands are soft and pulpy, their abdomens are prominent and jelly-like. When they run a block for a train, they puff and blow like disordered gasoline autos. Men get into this condition because they sit still too much; because they eat more than they need, and because they drink. No one gets into this condition because he wishes to. It is against the wish of everyone to have his body in this kind of order. He well knows that it lessens his working capacity, that it takes away a great deal of the fun of living; that it prevents his enjoying vigorous things as he did when a young man; and that it will probably cut off years at the end of his life. The reason that he does not come out of this condition is that he thinks it will involve a serious modification of his mode of living, a serious alteration of his business habits. He thinks it will involve

No. 1—The way in which squeezing intensly uses many muscles is beauti-
fully shown here.   The model has rolled up a wad of paper and is squeezing it as hard as he can.

doing an hour or two of monotonous exercise in a gymnasium every day.

Every man would like to have a firm hand, strong, clean-cut arms, muscles that stand out, a body that is solid, held together by firm muscles, strong vigorous neck, and large chest. A man cannot very well change the shape of the bones of his body; but aside from this, much can be done in a very short time every day. A month or two of work will help much to bring about that shape of the body that one desires, and that character of muscle which is one of the marks of vigorous manhood.

It is the purpose of this book to show how business men may, by a few minutes each day, develop their muscles in the way that they desire. That which is discussed in this article is not a complete system of physical training. This work does not aim to make a man graceful; it does not aim to make him a long distance runner, a jumper, or a fencer. This plan of exercise does succeed in almost every case, in quickly making a man muscularly strong and well developed. It does tend to make a man stand straighter, to respect himself more, to have a clearer

No. 2—Exercises of contracting the hand, if they are always followed by exercises by extending the fingers, which are shown in this picture, will never leave the hand in bad position. The delicate modeling of the muscles of the forearm is admirably shown.

head and better body. It does not take any apparatus —it can be done anywhere; it takes but little time. All that it demands is the willingness to do it on the part of the man. Many men have, in a single month, changed the whole appearance of their bodies from one of weakness to one of strength, from a condition of flabbiness to a condition of solidity. It is a common achievement for a man to increase the girth of his upper arm half an inch, or even an inch, in a month; to put two inches on his chest in the same length of time. If a man's muscles are fat to begin with, he may expect in the course of a month, to make them hard and muscular. In this case he will not expect to increase the size, as much as he will if his arms are merely soft to begin with and he has simply to build up.

THE ARMS.

We will begin with an explanation of how to develop the arms. Ordinarily, in the gymnasium one pulls against weights running over a pulley, or he lifts dumb bells, the object being to furnish resistance for the muscles to work against; good results are

No. 3—The blurring of the hands in this illustration is due to the trembling which is caused by the intense effort which is being made. The model well shows the powerful contraction of the muscles as far down as the waist. The beautiful modeling of the shoulder muscle, the deltoid, and of the muscles of the back which move the scapula, or shoulder blade, are rarely exhibited as finely as in this cut.

secured in this way; but to get the biggest development in the most rapid way, the muscles should be
contracted *to the full extent of their ability* every
time. A few contractions that are just as strong as
a man can make, will count more in the development
of size and also of strength than a very large number
of contractions of a moderate kind. Everyone uses
his hands a great deal, and yet the forearm does not
grow large and strong. The reason is that a great
deal of long continued moderate use does not develop
the muscles as much in size as a few exercises of the
intense kind.

It is a common experience for people working all
the winter in a gymnasium, working faithfully for
an hour three times a week, to expect they will have
increased their measurements very much; they are
frequently disappointed to find that their measurements have remained about the same. It is true, the
muscles are harder than they were before, they sleep
and digest their food better than before, but they had
expected a big gain in size of the arms, chest and body
muscles. The trouble in all these cases is that they
do not take the kind of exercise that is adapted to

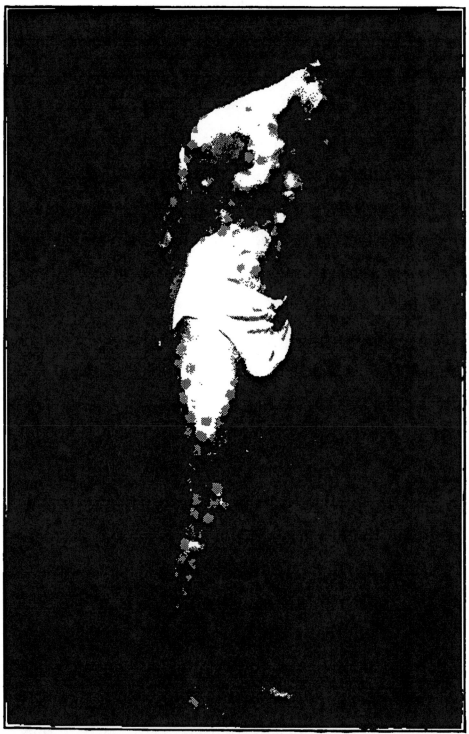

No. 4—In this exercise, the muscles of the front of the body, particularly the abdomen, are being contracted vigorously. Every one who does this exercise vigorously, should do twice as many in which the muscles of the back are contracted; the over-development of the muscles of the front of the body tends to make the individual round shouldered and flat chested.

building up muscular size; they took the exercise that is adapted to building up health. It is not at all true that there is any one kind of exercise that will accomplish all the known results to be obtained from exercise, any more that it is true that there is any one medicine which will accomplish all the results to be expected of medicine. One may exercise in order to become graceful in walking and moving about; one may exercise in order to become skillful in fencing, boxing, base ball or athletics; one may exercise in order to reduce fat; exercise may be taken in order to increase the activity of sluggish liver, and so on; but in each case if the results are to be secured, exercise must be adapted to the particular objects in mind. Thus, there is no such thing as a best exercise or as best exercises. The object of the exercises described in this article, is to increase the size and strength of the muscles. There is no attempt to increase their endurance or the skill with which one can use them.

These exercises do not directly aim to increase the health of the body, although this usually follows to some extent.

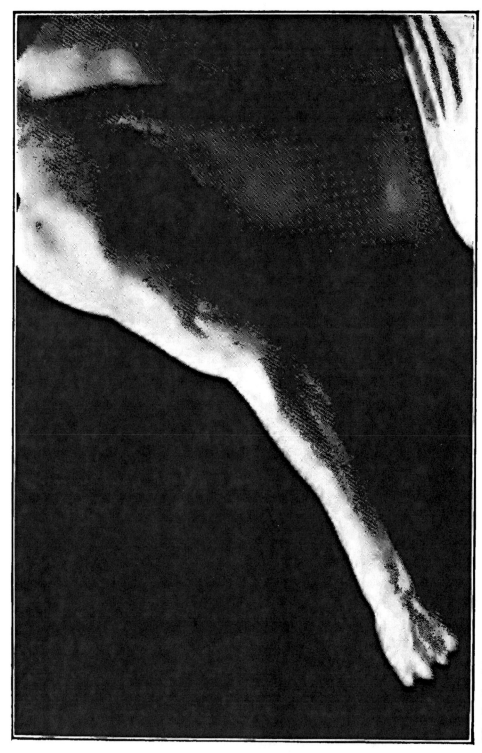

No. 5—In this photograph the action of the triceps or large muscle on the back of the arm is well shown. When the biceps is contracted hard, this muscle can be contracted and thus balance the effort of the triceps.

The fundamental principle is that from the muscles shall be demanded as great power as possible; a hundred movements of a light character will not build up muscle as rapidly as five movements of great effort. This is a general principle and applies to all the muscles of the body.

One of the old statements of the evolutionists is that "function makes structure"—this is one of the great guides in physical training. The kind of exercise that demands a given structure will in general, if persisted in, give that structure. For example: to pound with a hammer all day does not demand big muscles, so that the result of the exercise is to secure endurance rather than size and strength; on the other hand, to put up a hundred-pound bell does not demand endurance, but size and strength; so the result of putting up a hundred-pound bell is increase of size and strength. In the gymnasium one rarely pulls to the full extent of his power, because he cannot tell exactly how much weight he can lift, nor are the pulley weights adapted to heavy weights.

The plan here described is to have the muscles pull against each other. Thus it is easy to have them work

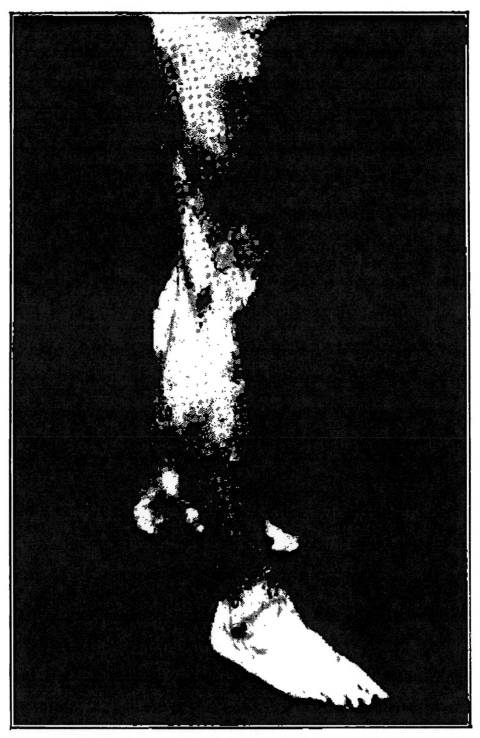

No. 6—An illustration of the front of the thigh showing how the muscle comes down and terminates abruptly.

to their utmost capacity without straining them; for example: in illustration No. 7 the model is using the muscles that clinch his hand as hard as possible, and at the same time is contracting the muscles that open his hand; the result is that the hand stays half way open, the fingers are rigidly fixed, the tendons of the wrist are prominent, the fore-arm is hard. This exercise repeated fifteen to twenty times in the morning, the same number of times at night, and a few times occasionally as a man is walking along the street by day, will do more to increase the size of the muscles of the forearm than all the hand-shaking, hand-writing, handling knife and fork, etc., that a man will do all day.) And more than this, a carpenter who is handling tools eight hours a day will not develop so big or so strong a forearm as will the man who takes this method. The long continued exercise with the hammer, saw and plane does not produce as strong contraction, and hence does not build up as large tissues, as this intense work that is done through the antagonistic muscles.

You will notice when you do this exercise as hard as possible, that the fingers and even the whole fore-

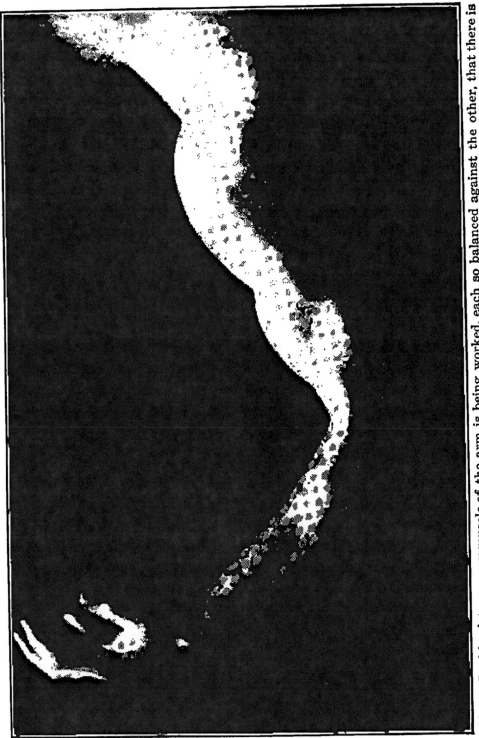

No. 7—In this picture every muscle of the arm is being worked, each so balanced against the other, that there is no movement, only a general trembling.

arm will shake with the intensity of the effort. This is the reason for the term *vibratory*. The position should be held under extreme contraction about three seconds, then the muscles should be allowed to become soft and the hand should be dropped. In about three seconds more the exercise should be repeated. The tendency will be not to work sufficiently hard at first. Every ounce of power that you have must be put into it, if you are going to gain more power. It is only by the investment of what you have, that you will gain more. Nature gives only what is necessary—if you make a demand upon your muscles for more power than you have, nature will gradually give it to you; but if you do not use what you have to the fullest extent, you will not be given much increase.

A few moments ago, I said that each exercise should not be continued for more than three seconds, and that then the muscles should be relaxed. The reason for this is that the circulation may be helped. When a muscle becomes hard by vigorous contraction, it tends to force out all the blood and lymph that is in it. New blood enters in under greater difficulties than under normal conditions; for this reason the

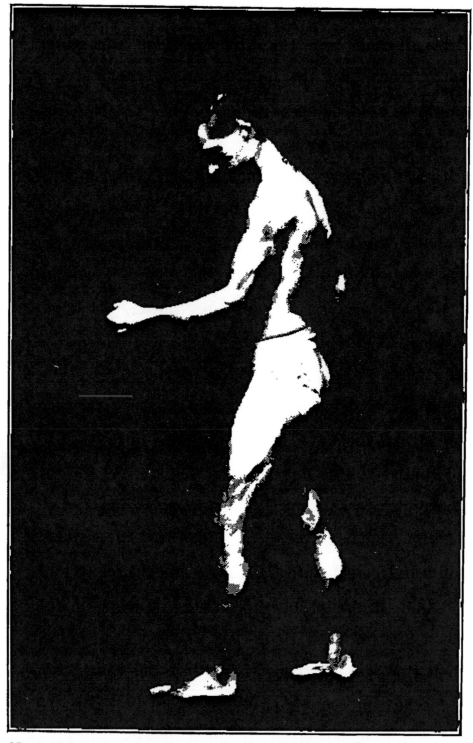

No. 8—Holding a wad of paper in the hand and squeezing it with all one's power for two or three seconds, is an excellent method for developing the whole arm. Its effect is well shown in the picture.

exercise should not be long in duration. The muscles should be allowed to become soft again. In order to favor its accomplishment a number of vigorous exercises rather short in duration should be taken.

One common way of exercising the forearm is to put something in the palm and grip it, a rubber ball, a piece of wood, or even a wad of paper. (Cut Nos. 1 and 8). The trouble with this exercise is two-fold; first, it develops only one set of muscles, the flexors, and the muscles that extend the fingers are left undeveloped; secondly, as a result of the development of the flexing muscles, and the non-development of the extensors, the hand when not in use tends to hang with the fingers almost closed into the palm (No. 9). The strong muscles have overbalanced the weak ones so that the hand is held nearly shut. By the method that I have proposed, flexors and extensors are developed together, and no matter how strong the forearm becomes, the hand and fingers will hang in a normal position.

The question may naturally be asked as to why I have said that gripping with the hand or exercising in some other way the muscles of the forearm with the greatest vigor will result in developing the muscles

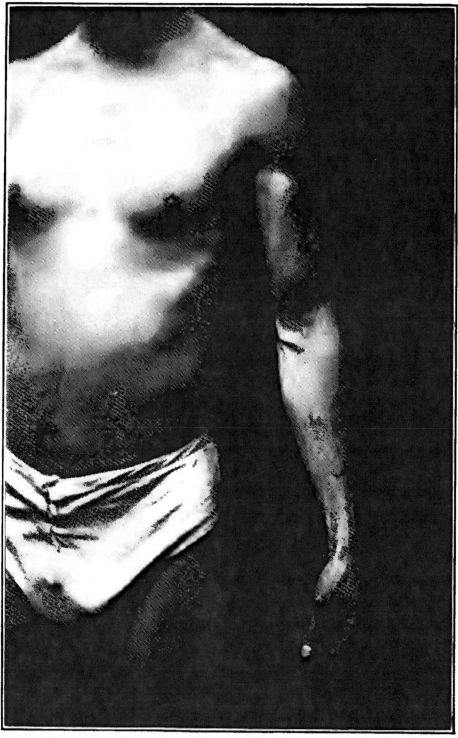

No. 9—A person who continues an exercise which developes the hand too much will soon acquire a hand which hangs, as is shown in the accompanying illustration; this is ungraceful and clumsy.

of the upper arm and the chest. The reason is this: the muscles which close the hand are, some of them, attached to the forearm, thus the tendons have to pass through the wrist. In order that they may work efficiently it is necessary that the wrist be held rigid. You cannot possibly clinch your hand hard and have the wrist free of movement. Now, in order to have the wrist held in a rigid position, all the muscles running from it up to the forearm (and some of them run to the lower part of the upper arm), must be contracted with great vigor. The elbow joint must also be held rigid, for the muscles which attach to the upper arm could not act efficiently were their points of origin movable. so it is necessary for the muscles which control the elbow to be contracted vigorously. These muscles, some of them, go up and attach to the shoulder blade and clavicle. So the muscles which hold the shoulder must be fixed in order that the big muscles of the chest and back may have solid support. The ribs have to be fixed solidly. In order to fix the ribs solidly we have to stop breathing. When a person takes hold of anything with the hand and squeezes it as hard as possible, he holds his breath.

No. 10--If the muscles are pressed deeply after the exercise, it will benefit them.

If this exercise is tried in front of a looking-glass one will see that gripping can be done to a moderate extent without contracting the muscles of the upper arm. So that when one squeezes as hard as possible, practically all the muscles of the arm and body are involved. This is the reason why squeezing of the hand as hard as possible will result in the development of the arm and shoulder as well. (Nos. 1 and 8.)

I have explained this exercise somewhat fully, as it is a type of all the others. All the exercises that are mentioned are exercises in which one group of muscles is pitted against its natural opponent, so that both are exercised to their fullest extent. You will find that to contract these muscles of the forearm as intensely as possible will involve the stiffening of the whole arm, and, indeed, of the upper part of the body. Always put your attention upon the particular part where you wish the chief effect. You will find, also, that you cannot contract these muscles with the greatest power without holding the breath; accordingly, before beginning the exercise it is well to take half a dozen breaths just as deep as you can; first blow out all the air possible from the chest and

No. 11—After the various muscles have been gone over as in the preceding illustration, the muscles should be slapped; this effort gives a stimulating effect which has most excellent results. One should slap all the muscles of the body; the model is merely slapping his arms.

then inhale to the fullest extent. Repeat this three or four times and then begin. If this deep breathing makes you a little dizzy the first few days, it shows that you need the exercise very much. The dizziness is to be overcome simply by persistence. Take deep breaths just up to the point where you begin to feel dizzy and then stop. It will not be many days before you can do all the deep breathing that you want to without feeling dizzy.

Having done the preliminary deep breathing take a deep breath and hold it while you do the first exercise, which consists of contracting the fingers of the hand for three seconds. Then let the breath go, and also let the fingers relax; take another deep breath and contract the hand muscles again. Repeat this ten times. The whole exercise ought to take one minute. Then with the right hand, squeeze the muscles of the left arm from the wrist to the elbow quickly; with the left hand similarly treat the right arm. Then slap the left arm from the wrist to the elbow. Follow this with similar treatment of the right. (See cuts 10 and 11.)

You are now ready for the second exercise, which

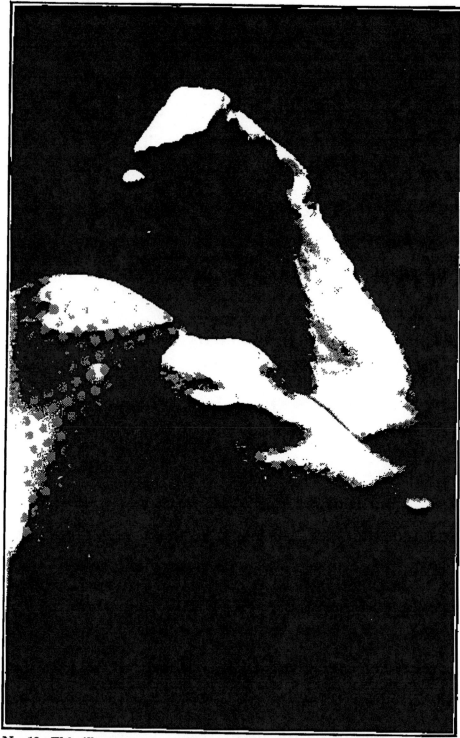

No. 12—This illustration was taken immediately following the preceding: the only difference in the two being, that in this case the palm is facing the shoulder, while in the other case the palm is away from the shoulder. The far greater contraction of the biceps with the palm toward the shoulder is already shown. When this muscle is being measured, it should always be contracted in this way, for otherwise it will appear to be much smaller than it really is.

is to exercise and develop the upper arm. The hand is to be placed in a similar position to that which was taken when the muscles of the forearm were to be exercised. But now the attention is to be fixed upon the biceps, the large muscle which shows on the front of the upper arm. It is to be contracted against the triceps, the muscles on the back of the arm, as hard as is possible. The biceps is well shown in Nos. 12 and 13. Some also show the contraction of the hand occurring at the same time. In the model (No. 5), the biceps are being strained against the muscles on the back of the arm. The same preliminary deep breathing should be taken in this case, and indeed in every case. The exercise should be repeated ten times as before. There is little use in doing the exercise unless one is going to put into it all the effort possible.

In some of the pictures that are shown, the outlines of the hand are a trifle blurred; the reason for this is that in spite of the most rapid exposure that it was possible to make indoors, with a specially prepared camera, it was impossible not to show the vibration of the hands under the intense effort that

No. 13—The little bunch near the elbow well shows the small muscles which turn the palm toward the shoulder. It also shows in excellent form the construction of the biceps in the forward part of the arm and of the triceps on the back of the arm pulling against the biceps.

was being made by the model. Illustrations Nos.
5 and 7 show the triceps on the back of the upper
arm as it is pulling against the biceps.

The next part of the body to be exercised is the
shoulder. This is best done at the same time that the
upper back is being developed. Illustrations Nos. 3
and 15 show these muscles in most vigorous contraction. The muscle on top of the shoulder, the deltoid,
and the great surface muscle of the upper back are
pulling the shoulder up and lifting the arm; while
the great muscles of the chest are pulling the arm
forward, and the other fibres of the trapezius are
pulling the shoulder back and down. The result is
that the shoulders and arms are set as if in iron.
These great masses of muscles, pulling with all their
inherent force, bind the joints together with the
greatest solidity. The illustrations show well the
contraction of these muscles. The extent to which
this contraction is carried on over other joints is
well shown. The double line of muscle extending
half way down the middle of the back shows two
muscles which pull the shoulder together; their development is well shown in No. 3. The tremen-
dous sweep of the great band of muscle coming from

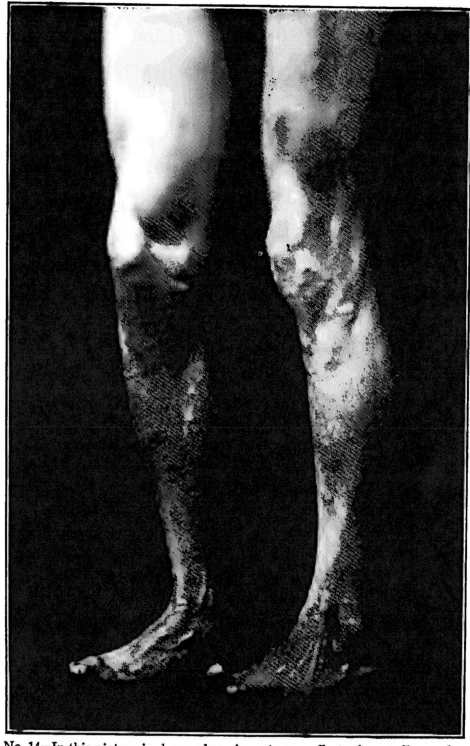

No. 14—In this picture is shown, how in extreme effort, the small muscles which lift the toes, are exceedingly active. The tendons on the back of the foot which stand out, are being pulled with great vigor.

the lower back, winding over the edge of the scapula, and then forward and upward to the upper arm, is superbly shown. This is the latissimus dorsi, the most powerful muscle that we have, by which we pull the arms down to the sides. This is effective in "chinning" one's self.

Taking a full breath, place yourself in this position as rigidly as possible for two or three seconds, then relax, and take a second breath easily, then another full breath, and repeat the exercise; pull the muscles with the utmost power that you possess. You will find it necessary to stiffen the neck and hold it well back. Remember that the shape of the body when it is being exercised vigorously is the shape that it tends to take during rest; so always exercise in positions that are strong and erect. Some of the illustrations show the contractions of the muscles on the front part of the body. These are given as type-forms rather than as the most desirable of positions for much exercise. *Exercises in which the back and neck are held rigidly erect, tend toward better carriage and should be taken about twice as frequently as exercises that pull the body forward.*

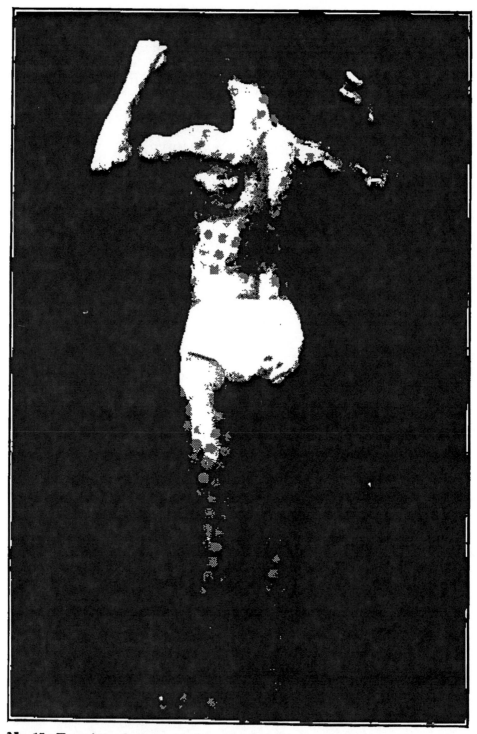

No. 15—Exercise of the muscles of the upper extremities and of the upper part of the body. The shading of color about the edge of the shoulder blade is the remains of a Summer's tan rather than the difference in muscle.

Illustration No. 16 shows well the exercise of the thigh. The great muscles that extend the legs are being contracted with the greatest vigor so that they stand out in massive folds. Most men walk quite a little; the result is that the average man has better legs than he has arms. These muscles are fully developed in many men, who otherwise are pretty flabby. It is well to bend the knee, hip and ankle joints a little. Then slowly contract the muscles to your utmost power until they stand out under the skin like piles of coiled rope, or like steel bands under the pressure of intense strain. After contracting the muscles of one thigh ten times, contract the muscles of the other thigh, similarly and an equal number of times.

Illustration No. 17 shows well the contraction of the great muscles which flex the leg on the thigh. These muscles do not show particularly well in ordinary use. The exercise should be carried out on both sides of the body. Nos. 3 and 19 show the great muscles of the lower back in active contraction: also show how the muscles of the forearm, upper arm and shoulder are working at the same time. The

No. 16—This illustration is to show the contraction of the "quadriceps extensor femoris," which is the large muscle at the front of the thigh, immediately above the knee. It shades off into a heavy flat tendon, which includes the knee cap. In the model the shadows to the left show where the belly of the muscle is shading off into the tendon. This muscle straightens the leg every time one raises up from having stooped to the floor. The straightening of the knee is accomplished by means of this muscle. It is one of the strongest muscles of the body.

fine lines running outward and downward from the spinal column show the intensity of the effort that is being made. The distended veins on the forearm are also indications of a similar character. This exercise should be carried on as are the others.

Illustrations Nos. 3 and 19 show exercises which are designed to be general—a large fraction of all the muscles of the body are working at once. In No. 18 the superficial muscle of the neck is shown in its great activity.

There is one danger to which these general exercises are exposed, that is, when so many muscles are used at once in such a vigorous way, the blood pressure of the body is increased with great rapidity. If the exercises are done excessively, the heart will be made irritable and sometimes over-developed. I have known a number of persons who, seeing the good effects of these exercises, have concluded that if the amount prescribed in these exercises would be good, twice as much would be twice as good, and have overdone the matter seriously. My father was once prescribing for an Hawaiian chief to whom he gave some pills, with instructions to take one three times

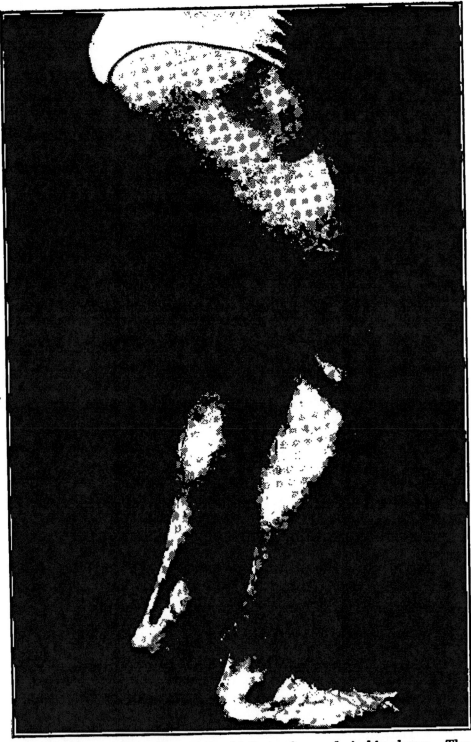

No. 17—The great muscles of the thigh are here admirably shown. The muscles which extend the thigh being on the front, and those which flex it being on the back. The knotted character of these muscles is well shown.

a day. He was so much benefited by the first that he concluded to take the whole box the following morning. His life was saved with great difficulty.

Another general caution in the use of these exercises needs to be given, and that is that beneficial effects are not usually secured by those who have completely passed the growing period. I should never encourage a man of over fifty to expect to profit by such exercises, and a man over forty should expect less than the young man may. Big girth of mucle is to be secured with advantage only during years when the body is at its maximum of efficiency.

Before undertaking to carry out this system of exercises, several things should be done. First determine how long it will be carried out; plan perhaps for one month, or at any rate, some definite period, otherwise one's resolution is apt to weaken and one will gradually do less and less, thinking to continue it when it is easier and business is not so pressing. This is usually an absolute fallacy. Men stop and do not begin it again. The thing to do is to undertake a definite plan. One month is a good length of time to undertake. It is long enough to

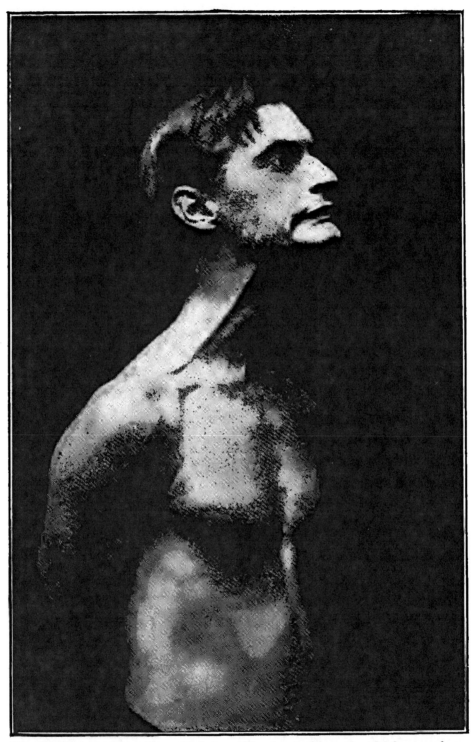

No. 18—Platysma myodies: This is a thin sheet of muscle which runs from the lower face down to the front of the body. Many animals have a corresponding muscle over most of the body. They can twitch their skin all over, just as we can twitch the skin of the neck. The skin of the chest can be pulled up nearly an inch, after one has become a little practised in the use of this muscle as a whole.

tax the will of most men; it is short enough to be within the ability of most men; it affords time enough to secure results which should be ample encouragement for continuation for another month.

Second, having settled the length of time that the programme will be followed out, next determine absolutely how much time each day, and at what time these exercises will be carried on. Ten minutes in the morning will do, but ten minutes in the morning and night will do more. It will be well to make a written record of one's purposes.

Third, measure the girth of your forearm, upper arms contracted (cuts Nos. 12 and 20), and straight, chest contracted and expanded, waist, thigh and neck. If you can get these measurements taken by someone who is familiar with such work, they will be accurate and satisfactory. You should have your measurements taken again at the end of the month in exactly the same way that they were taken at the beginning. They should, of course, be taken without any clothing on, that is, next to the skin, otherwise they will be quite unreliable. Arm should be as in No. 12 when measured, not No. 20.

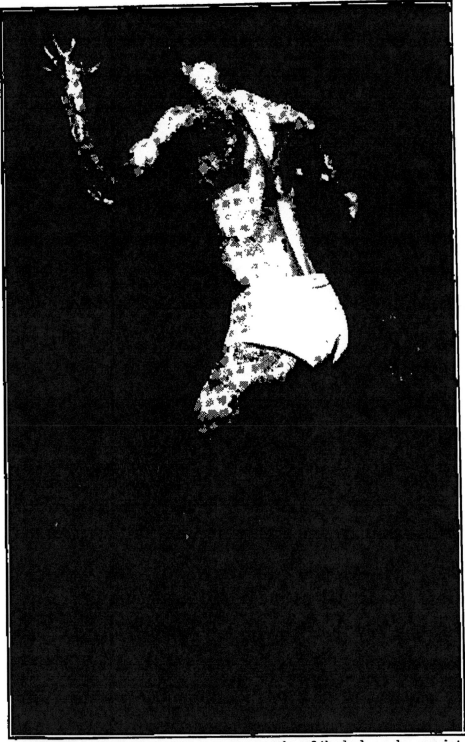

No. 19—The model is throwing as many muscles of the body as he can into action at once. The straining of the muscles of the forearm, upper arm and shoulder, and also right leg, show peculiarly well. This is one of the type of exercises which if long persisted in, tend to produce irritated heart, as it throws so much work upon the heart suddenly.

Fourth, select two exercisers on which to work. At the end of the month take two others. Nos. 8 and 6 make a good combination on which to start.

After the exercise, particularly in the morning, it is well to dip a towel in cool water, cold if it is pleasant, and pass it rapidly over the whole body. This should be followed by vigorous rubbing with a coarse towel. Get a silk crash towel, or even an ordinary crash towel of good length, and after you have been dried by the bath towel, use this over your body and limbs with the same vigor and speed that the modern shoe polisher exhibits when doing his work, until the whole body glows and feels the way your shoes look.

No. 20—The large muscle of the upper arm or the biceps. This muscle not only bends the forearm upon the upper arm, it also twists the forearm so that the palm faces the shoulder. In this illustration, the palm is away from the shoulder; and while the muscle is contracted vigorously, still the length of the muscle is evident. When the muscle is being measured it should be held as in cut No. 12.

THE FINEST EQUIPPED GYMNASIUM IN THE WORLD

The progress made in the manufacture and the mechanical perfection of the various gymnastic appliances shown in the complete gymnasium installed by A. G. Spalding & Bros. at the World's Fair, demonstrated that the firm is alive to the imperative need of the times. Physical training is being rapidly advanced and in the congested sections of the country it is a growing problem how to provide for the new conditions. This is particularly true in public school work and similar institutions. Real estate in large cities is extremely valuable, and as a consequence, gymnasiums are often reduced in size and wholly inadequate to the growing needs. This means that the apparatus of the past of a fixed or cumbersome character must be superseded by appliances that may be rapidly and conveniently handled in a manner to accommodate the constantly increasing number of boys and girls needing systematic physical development.

A. G. Spalding & Bros., who outfitted the complete gymnasium at the World's Fair and received the Grand Prize and Gold Medal in competition for their exhibit, are to be congratulated on their enterprise.

LIST OF APPARATUS INSTALLED IN WORLD'S FAIR GYMNASIUM.

20 No. OR Robert Reach Triplicate Chest Machines.
20 Special Rowing Attachments.
1 New Style Spalding Wrist Roll.
1 No. 50A Quarter Circle.
25 Sections Bar Stalls.
25 Bar Stall Benches.
2 No. 200 Neily Patent Bom.
6 Bar Saddles. and Vaulting Bars.
3 Special Combination Horizontal
1 Suspended Horizontal Bar—to swing up—Special.
1 No. 83 Low Parallel.
3 New Style Spalding Parallel Bars—Special.
3 No. 25 Jump Boards.
3 No. 0 Vaulting Horses.
3 Pairs Special Jump Stands.
3 Grasshopper Spring Boards.
3 No. 520 Storming Boards.
1 No. 207 Vaulting Box.
1 No. 28 Incline Board.
3 Pairs No. 125 Flying Rings.
8 No. 126 Traveling Rings.
12 No. 98 Climbing Ropes.
1 40-ft. Ladder and Braces.
1 Horizontal Window Ladder.
2 Vertical Window Ladders.
2 Striking Bag Discs and Bags.
11 5-ft. x 10-ft. x 2-in. Mats.
3 5-ft. x 6-ft. x 2-in. Mats.
3 3-ft. x 10-ft. x 2-in. Mats.
3 3-ft. x 5-ft. x 2-in. Mats.
1 Tumbling Mattress—5 ft. x 15 ft. x 8 in., curled hair.
2 Pairs Official Basket Ball Goals.
2 Pairs Official Screens for Basket Ball Goals.
2 No. M Official Basket Balls.
2 No. 1 Medicine Balls.
2 No. 2 Medicine Balls.
2 No. 3 Medicine Balls.
6 Medicine Ball Racks.
50 Pairs 1-2-lb. Model Dumb Bells.
50 Pairs 1-lb. Model Dumb Bells.
50 Pairs 1-lb. Indian Clubs.
50 Pairs 1 1-2-lb. Indian Clubs.
200 Pairs Club and Bell Hangers, on stands.
4 Dozen Wands.
4 Dozen. Bar Bells.
2 Wand Racks.
4 Dozen Savage Bar Bells.
8 Dozen Hangers for Bar Bells.
20 Head Gears.
20 Foot Gears.
1 Set Ring Hockey.
2 Sets Rope Quoits.
50 Bean Bags and Cabinet.
2 Sets Shuffleboard.
50 Rubber Balls and Cabinet.
4 8-ft. Jump Ropes.
4 20-ft. Jump Ropes.
1 Volley Ball Outfit.
4 Jump Frames.
50 Nickel Wands.
1 Wand Cabinet mounted on rollers for nickeled wands.
1 Game Cabinet.
50 Grace Hoops.
2 Grace Hoop Racks.
1 Pair Physician's Scales.
1 Stadiometer. [eter.
1 Chest, Back and Loin Dynamom-
1 Chinning Bar.
1 Pair Wall Parallels.
1 Chin Gauge.
1 Wet Spirometer.
1 Dozen Glass Mouth Pieces.
1 Pair Chest Calipers.
1 Pair Shoulder Calipers.
1 Spirometer—shelf.
1 Dynamometer for Grip.

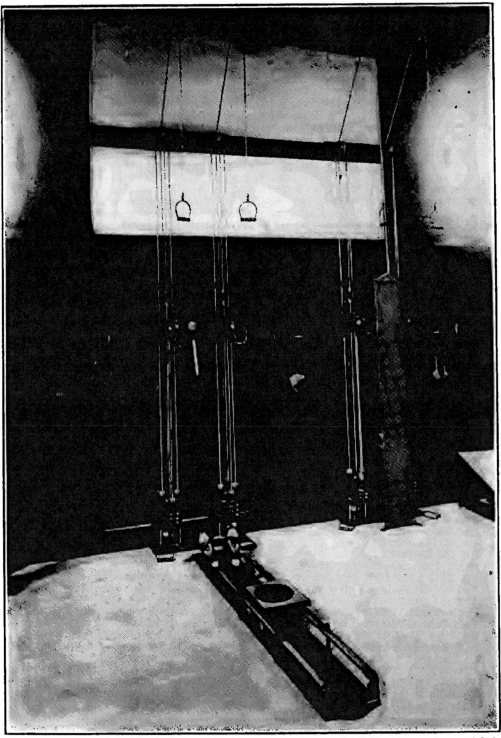

CUT No. 1—The above is a combination piece of wall apparatus which may be used as a rowing weight, back and loin pulley, direct chest pulley with upright backboard, or intercostal overhead pulleys. Either set of handles is always ready for use, and requires no adjustment.

CUT NO. 2—A portable Indian club and dumb bell rack, made of oak, mounted on rubber-tired wheels. The particular feature about it is the locking device, whereby an entire row of Indian clubs or dumb bells may be locked or unlocked with one throw of the lever, the object of the device being to place the control of the apparatus entirely in the hands of the instructor. The character of the hanger is decidedly unique and practical and is original with A. G. Spalding & Bros.

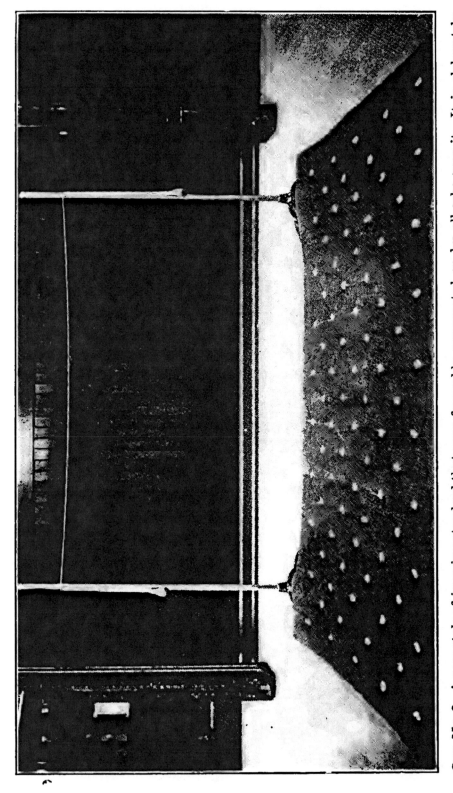

CUT NO. 3.—A new style of jumping standard that was favorably commented on by all who saw it. It is elaborately made of polished brass tubing and brass fittings, having a heavy iron round base. The particular feature of its construction was the automatic pin arrangement which was permanently attached to the standard and was instantly adjusted, locking itself when released at the desired height.

CUT No. 4—Shows a combined horizontal and vaulting bar of entirely
new construction. The bars are suspended by overhead guys
and these guys are tightened and the bar drawn into position
at the floor by the use of one lever on each upright. The principle is radically new, and is certainly most successfully ap-
plied. The bar requires only two floor plates and two points
of attachment at the floor, eliminating the spread of guys, thereby
saving floor space and greatly facilitating the handling of the
apparatus in clearing the floor for other work.

CUT No. 5—Illustrates a pair of parallel bars, the design of which was particularly commended by the entire body of Turn Verein representatives who used them in the Olympic gymnastic contests.

CUT No. 6—A photograph from one end of the gymnasium showing considerable of the apparatus in place on the floor. The net in the centre of the room is for volley ball games. Owing to the character of the apparatus the floor may be quickly cleared for games of this character at short notice.

IRON DUMB BELLS

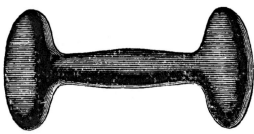

Made on approved models, nicely balanced and finished in black enamel. Sizes, 2 to 40 lbs. Per lb., **6c.**

Over 40 lbs., **8c.** per lb.

Bar Bells, any weight, with wrought iron handle, any

length made specially. . . . . . . Per lb., **10c.**

NICKEL=PLATED DUMB BELLS

Nickel-plated and
    polished.

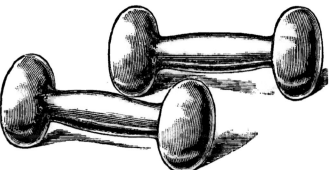

No.		Per Pair
1N.	1 lb.,	$ .25
2N.	2 "	.50
3N.	3 "	.65
4N.	4 "	.75
5N.	5 "	1.00

NICKEL=PLATED DUMB BELLS
WITH RUBBER BANDS

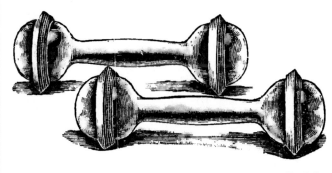

Nickel-plated and
    polished.

No.		Per Pair
1B.	1 lb.,	$ .65
2B.	2 "	.75
3B.	3 "	1.00
4B.	4 "	1.15
5B.	5 "	1.25

Handsomely illustrated catalogue mailed free to any address.

A. G. SPALDING & BROS.

New York	Chicago	Philadelphia	San Francisco
St. Louis	Boston	Buffalo	Baltimore
Denver	Minneapolis	Kansas City	Montreal, Can.

London, England

Spalding's
Trade-Mark Wood Dumb Bells

Our Trade-Mark Bells are made of selected material, neatly decorated, well finished and of perfect balance.

1-4 pound.	.	Per pair, $ .40
1-2 pound.	.	" .40
3-4 pound.	.	" .45
1 pound.	.	" .50
1 1-2 pound.	.	" .55
2 pound.	.	" .65
3 pound.	.	" .90
4 pound.	.	" 1.10

Trade Line Wood Dumb Bells

NOT TRADE-MARK QUALITY

1-4 pound.	.	Per pair, 25c.
1-2 pound.	.	" 25c.
3-4 pound.	.	" 30c.
1 pound.	.	" 35c.
1 1-2 pound.	.	" 40c.
2 pound.	.	" 45c.
3 pound.	.	" 55c.
4 pound.	.	" 70c.

Spalding's handsomely illustrated catalogue of athletic goods mailed free to any address.

A. G. SPALDING & BROS.

New York	Chicago	St. Louis	Washington	San Francisco
Boston	Minneapolis	Baltimore	Kansas City	Montreal, Can.
Buffalo	Philadelphia	Denver	Pittsburg	London, England

Spalding's Trade-Mark Indian Clubs

Our Trade-Mark Indian Clubs are of selected material and perfect in shape. They are finely polished, with ebonite centre band and gilt stripe top and bottom. Each pair wrapped in paper bag.

1-2 pound............................Per pair, $ .40
3-4 pound............................ " .45
1 pound............................ " .50
1 1-2 pound............................ " .55
2 pound............................ " .65
2 1-2 pound............................ " .80
3 pound............................ " .90
4 pound............................ " 1.10
5 pound............................ " 1.40

Trade Line Indian Clubs

The following clubs are not Trade-Mark goods, but of good material and far superior in shape and finish to the ordinary clubs on the market.

1-2 pound............................Per pair, 25c.
3-4 pound............................ " 30c.
1 pound............................ " 35c.
1 1-2 pound............................ " 40c.
2 pound............................ " 45c.
2 1-2 pound............................ " 50c.
3 pound............................ " 55c.
4 pound............................ " 70c.
5 pound............................ " 90c.

Spalding's handsomely illustrated catalogue of athletic goods mailed free to any address.

A. G. SPALDING & BROS.

New York	Chicago	St. Louis	Washington	San Francisco
Boston	Minneapolis	Baltimore	Kansas City	Montreal, Can.
Buffalo	Philadelphia	Denver	Pittsburg	London, England

Special Award and Grand Prize

Spalding Gymnasium Shoes

Low cut, best grade canvas shoe; white rubber sole; in ladies' and men's sizes; men's made of white canvas, ladies' black.

No. 1. Pair, $1.25

Low cut canvas shoe, with rubber sole.

No. K. Pair, 75c.

Low cut canvas, canvas sole; very popular for gymnasium.

No. E. Pair, 35c.

A. G. SPALDING & BROS.

New York	Chicago	St. Louis	Washington	San Francisco
Boston	Minneapolis	Baltimore	Kansas City	New Orleans
Buffalo	Philadelphia	Denver	Pittsburg	Syracuse
Cincinnati		Montreal, Can.		London, England

Special Award and Grand Prize

Spalding Gymnasium Shoes

Selected leather, electric sole.   A very easy and
flexible shoe.

No. **20.**   Low Cut.   Per pair, **$1.50**
No. **21.**   High Cut.   "   **1.75**

Low cut shoe, selected leather, extra light and
elkskin sole; in ladies' and men's sizes.

No. **166.**   Per pair, **$2.50**

A. G. SPALDING & BROS.

New York	Chicago	St. Louis	Washington	San Franiscco
Boston	Minneapolis	Baltimore	Kansas City	New Orleans
Buffalo	Philadelphia	Denver	Pittsburg	Syracuse
	Cincinnati	Montreal, Can.		London, England

SPECIAL AWARD AND GRAND PRIZE

were won by A. G. SPALDING & BROS. at the Louisiana Purchase Exposition, 1904, for the best, most complete and most attractive installation of Gymnastic Apparatus and Athletic Supplies shown at the World's Fair.

Spalding Gymnasium Shoes

Horsehide sole; soft and flexible; in ladies' and men's sizes.

No. 155.   Pair, $3.50

Kangaroo; elkskin sole, extra light, hand made.

No. 15.   Pair, $4.00

High cut, best grade canvas shoe, white rubber sole; in ladies' and men's sizes; men's made of white canvas, ladies' black.

No. 1H.   Pair, $1.50

High cut canvas shoe, rubber sole.

No. M. Pair, $1.00

A. G. SPALDING & BROS.

New York	Chicago	St. Louis	Washington	San Francisco
Boston	Minneapolis	Baltimore	Kansas City	New Orleans
Buffalo	Philadelphia	Denver	Pittsburg	Syracuse
Cincinnati		Montreal, Can.		London, England

SPECIAL AWARD AND GRAND PRIZE

BASKET BALL SHOE

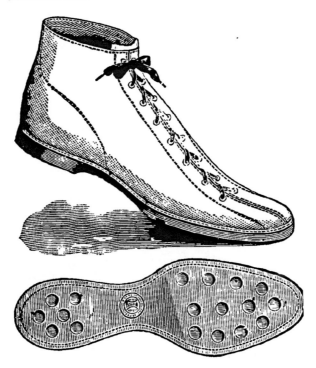

Made of selected leather with special rubber sole.
The suction caused by the peculiar construction of
the sole enables the player to obtain a good purchase
on the floor, a feature that should make this shoe
very popular with basket ball players.

No. BB. Per pair, **4.00**

For ladies; otherwise same as No. BB.

No. BBL. Per pair, **$3.50**

SPECIAL AWARD AND GRAND PRIZE

Spalding's New Regulation Hammer With Wire Handle

Lead   EACH
No. 9. 12-lb., Lead, Practice, $4.25
No. 10. 16-lb., Lead, Regulation, 4.50

Iron   EACH
No. 12. 8-lb., Iron, Juvenile, $2.50
No. 14. 12-lb., Iron, Practice, 3.00
No. 15. 16-lb., Iron, Regulation, 3.25

Extra Wire Handles   EACH
No. 6H. For above hammers, 50c.

Shot

No. 19. 16-lb., Lead. Each, $2.50
No. 21. 12-lb., Lead.   "   2.25
No. 23. 16-lb., Iron.   "   1.75
No. 25. 12-lb., Iron.   "   1.50
No. 18.   8-lb., Iron.   "   1.25

A. G. SPALDING & BROS.

New York	Chicago	St. Louis	Washington	San Francisco
Boston	Minneapolis	Baltimore	Kansas City	New Orleans
Buffalo	Philadelphia	Denver	Pittsburg	Syracuse
Cincinnati		Montreal, Can.		London, England

SPECIAL AWARD AND GRAND PRIZE

were won by A. G. SPALDING & BROS. at the Louisiana Purchase Exposition, 1904, for the best, most complete and most attractive installation of Gymnastic Apparatus and Athletic Supplies shown at the World's fair.

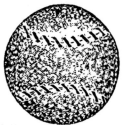

Indoor Shot

With our improved leather cover. Does not lose weight even when used constantly.

No. 3. 12-lb. Indoor Shot. Each, $7.00
No. 4. 16-lb. Indoor Shot. . . " 7.50
No. 26. 8-lb. Indoor Shot. . . " 5.00

Regulation 56-lb. Weights

Made after model submitted by Champion J. S. Mitchel, and endorsed by all weight throwers. Packed in box and guaranteed correct in weight and in exact accordance with rules of A. A. U.

No. 2
Lead 56-lb. Weights Complete, $8.50

SPECIAL AWARD AND GRAND PRIZE

INDOOR RUNNING SHOES
Made With or Without Spikes.

Fine leather, rubber tipped sole, with spikes.
No. 111.   Per pair, $3.50

Leather shoe, rubber tipped, with spikes.
No. 112.   Per pair, $3.00

Leather shoe, rubber tipped, no spikes.
No. 114.   Per pair, $2.50

INDOOR JUMPING SHOES

Best leather Indoor Jumping Shoe, hand-made, rubber soles.
No. 210.   Per pair, $5.00

A. G. SPALDING & BROS.

New York	Chicago	St. Louis	Washington	San Francisco
Boston	Minneapolis	Baltimore	Kansas City	New Orleans
Buffalo	Philadelphia	Denver	Pittsburg	Syracuse
Cincinnati		Montreal, Can.		London, England

SPECIAL AWARD AND GRAND PRIZE

were won by A. G. SPALDING & BROS. at the Louisiana Purchase Exposition, 1904, for the best, most complete and most attractive installation of Gymnastic Apparatus and Athletic Supplies shown at the World's fair.

Full Sleeve Shirts

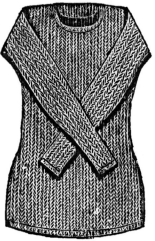

Best Worsted, full fashioned, stock colors and sizes.

No. 1D.   Each, $3.75

Cut Worsted, stock colors and sizes.

No. 602.   Each, $1.75

Cotton, Flesh, White and Black.

No. 3D.   Each, $1.00

Knee Tights

Best Worsted, full fashioned, stock colors and sizes.

No. 1B.   Per pair, $2.75

Cut Worsted, stock colors and sizes.

No. 604.   Per pair, $1.25

Sanitary Cotton, stock colors and sizes.

No. 4B.   Per pair, 50c.

A. G. SPALDING & BROS.

New York	Chicago	St. Louis	Washington	San Francisco
Boston	Minneapolis	Baltimore	Kansas City	New Orleans
Buffalo	Philadelphia	Denver	Pittsburg	Syracuse
Cincinnati		Montreal, Can.		London, England

Running Pants

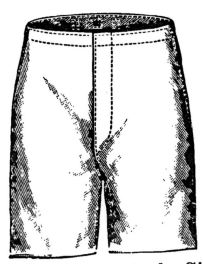

White or black Sateen, fly front, lace back.

No. 1.

Per pair, $1.25

White or black Sateen, lace back, fly front.

No. 2.

Per pair; $1.00

White or black Silesia fly front, lace back.

No. 3.

Per pair, 75c.

White or black Silesia, fly front, lace back.

No. 4.

Per pair, 50c.

White Silesia, fly front, lace back.

No. 6.

Per pair, 35c.

Stripes down sides of any of these running pants, 25 cents per pair extra.

Special Award and Grand Prize

were won by A. G SPALDING & BROS. at the Louisiana Purchase Exposition, 1904, for the best, most complete and most attractive installation of Gymnastic Apparatus and Athletic Supplies shown at the World's Fair.

Full Length Tights and Trousers

FULL
TIGHTS

Full Tights, best worsted, full fashioned, stock colors and sizes.

No. 1A, Per pair, $3.75

Full Tights, cut worsted, stock colors and sizes.

No. 605. Per pair, $2.00

Full Tights, cotton, full quality. White, Black, Flesh.

No. 3A. Per pair, $1.00

Y. M. C. A. TROUSERS

Regulation Style

REGULATION
Y. M. C. A. STYLE

No. 4. Flannel, medium quality. . .	Per pair, $1.75
No. 3. Flannel, good quality. . . .	" 2.50

Spalding's handsomely illustrated catalogue of athletic goods mailed free to any address.

A. G. SPALDING & BROS.

New York	Chicago	St. Louis	Washington	San Franiscco
Boston	Minneapolis	Baltimore	Kansas City	New Orleans
Buffalo	Philadelphia	Denver	Pittsburg	Syracuse
Cincinnati		Montreal, Can.		London, England

JIU JITSU

Spalding's Athletic Library
No. 233

Per Copy 10 Cents

A complete description of this famous Japanese system of self defence. Each move thoroughly explained and illustrated with numerous full page pictures of Messrs. A. Minami and K. Koyama, two of the most famous exponents of Jiu Jitsu in America, who posed especially for this book. Be sure to ask for Spalding's Athletic Library book on Jiu Jitsu.

How to Become a Boxer

Spalding's Athletic Library No. 162

For many years books have been issued on the art of boxing, but it has remained for us to arrange a book which we think is sure to fill all demands. It contains over 70 pages of illustrations showing all the latest blows, posed especially for this book under the supervision cf one of the best instructors of boxing in the United States, who makes a specialty of teaching and who knows how to impart his knowledge. They are so arranged that anyone can easily become a proficient boxer. The book also contains pictures of all the well-known boxers. A partial list of the 200 pages of the book include: A history of boxing; how to box; the correct position; the hands; clenching the fist; the art of gauging distance; the first principles of hitting; the elements of defence; feinting; knockout blows; the chin punch; the blow under the ear; the famous solar plexus knockout; the heart blow; f-mous blows and their originators; Fitzsimmons' contribution; the McCoy corkscrew; the kidney punch; the liver punch; the science of boxing; proper position of hand and arm; left hook to face; hook to the jaw; how to deliver the solar plexus; correct delivery of a right uppercut; blocking a right swing and sending a right uppercut to chin; blocking a left swing and sending a left uppercut to chin; the side step; hints on training, diet and breathing; how to train; rules for boxing.

Per Copy 10 Cents

285 HEALTH ANSWERS

BY PROF. E. B. WARMAN

SPALDING'S ATHLETIC LIBRARY No. 213

Contents: Necessity for exercise in the summer; three rules for bicycling; when going up-hill; sitting out on summer nights; ventilating a bedroom; ventilating a house; how to obtain pure air; bathing; salt water baths at home; a substitute for ice water; drinking ice water; to cure insomnia; asleep in two minutes; for those who ride wheels; summer outdoor exercise; profuse perspiration; danger of checking perspiration; dress, hot weather; light colored clothing; how to avoid catching cold; eating; a few good rules; drinking; how to go up and down stairs; the proper way to breathe; correct position; to secure correct position; the right way to sit; when you are walking; perfect freedom; stationary running; fish as brain food; condiments; internal baths; honey; anemic condition; high collars; alcohol; measurements of women; process of digestion; southern corn; children dining; blanched almonds; ice-cold water; beans; running; insomnia; consumptives; tub bath; codfish and potatoes; rheumatism; strength begins in the stomach; nervousness; poor complexions; lines about the mouth; sleeplessness and nervousness; school gymnastics; coffee; feats of strength; palpitation of the heart; measurements of men; catching cold easily; hoping against hope; sea salt; what is health? what is disease? strength from the earth; nutrition; winter underwear; quantity of air; in your athletic work; rub down after the bath; amount of food required; sleeping without a pillow; short windedness; woolen underwear; complexion tablets; bathing when tired; beauty; the brain worker; two meals a day; how often to exercise; mixed diet; nostril breathing; blushing; the lungs; sallow, or muddy complexion; facial muscles; draughts; vegetarians; a perfect woman; gray hair; eat less; stoop shouldered; eat more; varicose veins; offensive breath; offensive perspiration; consumption; animal foods; callous spots; to increase in weight; mixed diet necessary, diet essential; dreaming; repair and waste; water tub baths; osteopathy; swimming; diet essential; dreaming; repair and waste; fluttering of the heart; importance of ventilation; appendicitis; to overcome shortwindedness; French heels; the train skirt; flying all to pieces; longevity; bicycling; public speakers and singers; thinness; woolen underwear; starchy food; acid dyspepsia; bleaches; best time to bathe; daily needs of the body; skin blemishes; restaurant luncheons; active chest; the ankles; smoking; how to rest; cold feet; slenderness; hair tonics; cereals; diet; sugar; thin women; nervous indigestion; hearty breakfast; worry; shoulder braces; that tired feeling; obesity; the neck; paleness; tired limbs; sodium phosphate; proper insulation; cream or milk; massage; thin hair; dark circles; lemon juice; open air; waterproof dress; beneficial exercise; housework; swollen feet; mouth breathing; toilet soap; sunlight; massage; children; indigestion; black hats; carry your head high; playing golf; the brown streak; the hips; mastication; rope jumping; snoring; digestion; do not be deceived; liquids at meals; acid of lemons; fresh fruits; conservation; vapor baths; lung expansion; the bones; pronounced muscles; vigorous exercise; diabetes; sighing; carry the head; sipping water; abnormal acidity; lung expansion; double chin; cooked foods; consumptives; heredity; take nothing; rye; black specks; manipulation; all manicures; ether; pure toilet soaps; a rubber comb; the parched, etc.; the requirements of health; the weeping sinew; heavy bed clothing; feather pillows; dandruff; tired feet; all cereals; for tender feet; barley; one who is ill; large pores; internal baths; oats; the use of any drug; a cold water bath; sugar; excessive blood; all depilatories; consumptives; fresh fruits; wheat; rice; lettuce; health; an outing; cornmeal; an oily complexion; filtered water; boiling the water; distilled water; fruit for gout; the palms; skimmed milk; alcohol; buttermilk; vegetables; muscle food; cocoa butter; buttermilk as a skin lotion; men of sedentary habits; children; beef tea; timely suggestions; oatmeal; oil obtained; the best known remedy; dark circles; a weak heart; snuffing any liquid; brain food; the term proteid; rough red hands; curvature; cold water; apples; shortness of breath; sunburned faces; bones require food; laugh and grow fat; fat taken as food; very obese people; beans, the poor man's friend; when summer comes; prevention; excessive flesh; patience; a headache; plants; iron; blackheads; la grippe; flowers in bedroom; feed a cold; la grippe; children; power of thought; hard hitting; high altitude; eye exercises.

PRICE 10 CENTS

AMERICAN SPORTS PUBLISHING COMPANY, 15 WARREN STREET, NEW YORK

A SPECIAL AWARD AND A GRAND PRIZE

were won by A. G. SPALDING & BROS. at the Louisiana Purchase Exposition, 1904, for the best, most complete and most attractive installation of Gymnastic Apparatus, Base Ball and Athletic Supplies shown at the World's Fair.

THE SPALDING OFFICIAL LEAGUE BALL

Used exclusively by the National League, Minor Leagues, and by all Intercollegiate and other Associations for over a quarter of a century. Each ball wrapped in tinfoil and put in a separate box, and sealed in accordance with the regulations of the National League and American Association. Warranted to last a full game when used under ordinary conditions.

Each, $1.25

A. G. SPALDING & BROS.

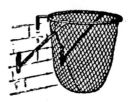

Ten Minutes' Exercise
By Dr. Luther Gulick **for Busy Men**

Dr. Gulick says: "The experience of years has demonstrated the efficiency of the exercises contained in 'Ten Minutes' Exercise for Busy Men' in securing the ends for which they were devised. Many letters have been written by men, testifying to the great benefit which they have secured from these few minutes of simple but vigorous work.

"* * * The correspondence schools of physical training have come into great activity. Their general aim is to build up big muscles. A somewhat careful investigation of them satisfies me that they are inferior to the exercises in this drill for purposes of building up vigor and manliness.

"One of the most vigorous claims of some of these schools, namely, that the heart particularly is benefited by their work, is false, for I have had case after case of men whose hearts have been injured by taking the correspondence schools' work when they were not in condition for it.

"The exercises in 'Ten Minutes' Exercise for Busy Men' are recommended with the confidence of long, successful use. The results secured are better than those possible from the correspondence school work in the specific directions mentioned."

PRICE BY
MAIL
10 CENTS

American
Sports
Publishing
Co.

16-18 Park
Place
New York

HOW TO BECOME A BOXER

For many years publications have been issued on the art of boxing that to a certain extent did not enable the novice nor the youth to become proficient in the manly art. There is probably no man in America better qualified to teach boxing than Prof. William Elmer, and in his book on the subject he goes into it very exhaustively. The book contains about seventy full page illustrations, showing how each blow is to be made, how to attack and how to defend yourself. It shows how the hands must be held and the positions to take, with descriptions that are so accurate that any boy can take them, open them up and with a young friend become proficient. Besides being a fully illustrated book on the art of self-defence, it contains nearly all the photographs of the leading American boxers and the positions they take, which in itself is instructive; the different rules under which all contests are held, and articles which will interest anyone on the question of physical education. In order to make this publication the most accurate one issued, Prof. Elmer had his sparring partner posed personally for all the illustrations.

PRICE BY MAIL 10 CENTS.

American Sports Publishing Co.

16–18 Park Place, New York.

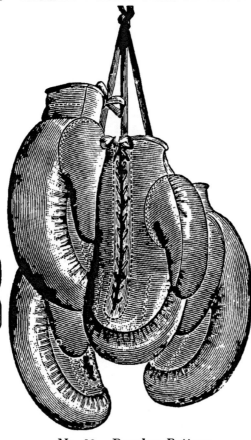

No. 23. Regular Pattern

Spalding Boxing Gloves

No. 9. Regulation 5 oz. glove, gambia tan leather, padded with best curled hair, patent palm lacing, padded wristband, patent palm grip. Substantially made throughout for hard usage. : : Per set, **$4.50**

No. 14. Regulation 5 oz. glove, dark wine color, padded wristband, patent palm lacing and palm grip. . Per set, **$3.25**

No. 23. Regular pattern, outer handpiece of olive tanned leather, grip and cuffs of darker shade, hair padded and patent palm lacing. . . . . Per set, **$1.50**

No. 24. Regular pattern, outer handpiece of dark wine color tanned leather, grip and cuffs of darker shade; hair padded, elastic wristband. . . . Per set, **$1.00**

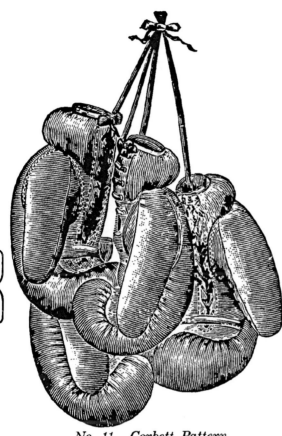

No. 11.   Corbett Pattern

SPALDING BOXING GLOVES

No. 11. Corbett pattern, large 7 oz. glove, gambia tan leather, padded with best curled hair, patent palm lacing, padded wrist band, patent palm grip. Substantially made throughout for hard usage. Per set, **$4.50**

No. 13. Corbett pattern, olive tanned leather, well padded with hair, patent palm lacing and patent palm grip. Per set, **$4.00**

No. 15. Corbett pattern, soft tanned leather, well padded with hair, padded wristband, patent palm lacing, patent palm grip. . Per set, **$3.00**

No. 17. Corbett pattern, craven tan leather, well padded with hair, patent palm lacing, patent palm grip, padded wristband.   Per set, **$3.00**

No. 19. Corbett pattern, craven tan leather, well padded with hair, patent palm grip and patent palm lacing.   .   .   Per set, **$2.50**

No. 21. Corbett pattern, grip and cuffs of olive tanned leather, balance of glove finished in dark wine color tanned leather. Well padded with hair and patent palm lacing.   .   .   .   Per set, **$2.00**

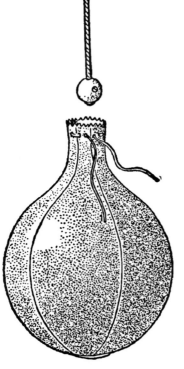

SPALDING'S ATHLETIC LIBRARY

Spalding's Athletic Library is devoted to all athletic sports and pastimes, indoor and outdoor, and is the recognized American cyclopedia of sport. Each book is complete in itself; and those sports which are governed by National Associations always designate Spalding's Athletic Library as the official publication. This gives to each book the official authority to contain the rules. Each year the books are brought up to date, with the latest rules, new ideas, new pictures and valuable information, thus making the series the most valuable of its kind in the world. The price, 10 cents per copy, places them in the reach of all, and no one's library can be complete unless all numbers are found therein.

No. 12—Association Foot Ball

Contains valuable information, diagrams of play, and rules for both the Gaelic and Association styles of play. Price 10 cents.

No. 13- How to Play Hand Ball

By the world's champion, Michael Egan, of Jersey City. This book has been rewritten and brought up to date in every particular. Every play is thoroughly explained by text and diagram. The numerous illustrations consist of full pages made from photographs of Champion Egan, showing him in all his characteristic attitudes. Price 10 cents.

No. 14—Curling

History of the sport; diagram of curling rink; rules for curling; diagrams of play. Price 10 cents.

No. 23—Canoeing

By C. Bowyer Vaux. Paddling, sailing, cruising and racing canoes and their uses; canoeing and camping. Price 10 cents.

No. 27—College Athletics

M. C. Murphy, the well-known athletic trainer, now with Yale University, the author of this book, has written it especially for the schoolboy and college man, but it is invaluable for the athlete who wishes to excel in any branch of athletic sport. The subjects comprise the following articles: Training, starting, sprinting; how to train for the quarter, half, mile and longer distances; walking; high and broad jumping; hurdling; pole vaulting; throwing the hammer. Illustrated. Price 10 cents.

No. 29—Exercising With Pulley Weights

By Dr. Henry S. Anderson, instructor in heavy gymnastics Yale gymnasium, Anderson Normal School, Chautauqua University. In conjunction with a chest machine anyone with this book can become perfectly developed. Contains all the various movements necessary to become proficient and of well-developed physique. Price 10 cents.

No. 40—Archery

By J. S. Mitchel. An introductory chapter on the use of the bow and arrow; archery of the present day; the bow and how to use it, with practical illustrations on the right and wrong method of aiming. Price 10 cents.

No. 55—Official Sporting Rules

Contains rules not found in other publications for the government of many sports; rules for wrestling, cross-country running, shuffleboard, skating, snowshoeing, quoits, potato racing, professional racing, racquets, pigeon flying, dog racing, pistol and revolver shooting. Price 10 cents.

No. 87—Athletic Primer

Edited by James E. Sullivan, Secretary-Treasurer of the Amateur Athletic Union; tells how to organize an athletic club, how to conduct an athletic meeting, and gives rules for the government of athletic meetings; contents also include directions for building a track and laying out athletic grounds, and a very instructive article on training; fully illustrated with pictures of leading athletes in action. Price 10 cents.

No. 102—Ground Tumbling

By Prof. Henry Walter Worth, who was for years physical director of the Armour Institute of Technology. Any boy, by reading this book and following the instructions, which are drawn from life, can become a proficient tumbler; all the various tricks explained. Price 10 cents.

No. 104—The Grading of Gymnastic Exercises

By G. M. Martin, Physical Director of the Y. M. C. A. of Youngstown, Ohio. It is a book that should be in the hands of every physical director of the Y. M. C. A., school, club, college, etc. The contents comprise: The place of the class in physical training; grading of exercises and season schedules—grading of men, grading of exercises, season schedules for various classes, elementary and advanced classes, leaders, optional exercises, examinations, college and school work; calisthenic exercises, graded apparatus exercises and general massed class exercises. Nearly 200 pages. Price 10 cents.

IN all athletic contests the implements and apparatus must conform to the official rules as laid down by the governing bodies of the various sports, the object being to enable all contestants to compete under uniform conditions and with the same kind of an implement, for a record in any sport will not be allowed unless the official implement is used. That is why Spalding implements are always selected, because they never vary in weight or measurement, but invariably conform to the rules. . . . . .

OFFI

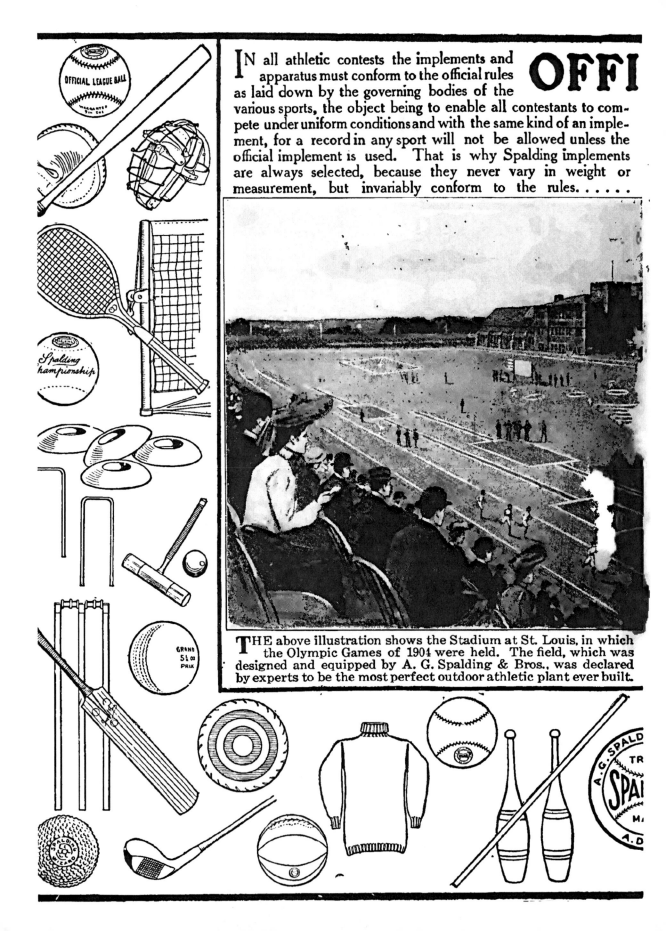

THE above illustration shows the Stadium at St. Louis, in which the Olympic Games of 1904 were held. The field, which was designed and equipped by A. G. Spalding & Bros., was declared by experts to be the most perfect outdoor athletic plant ever built.

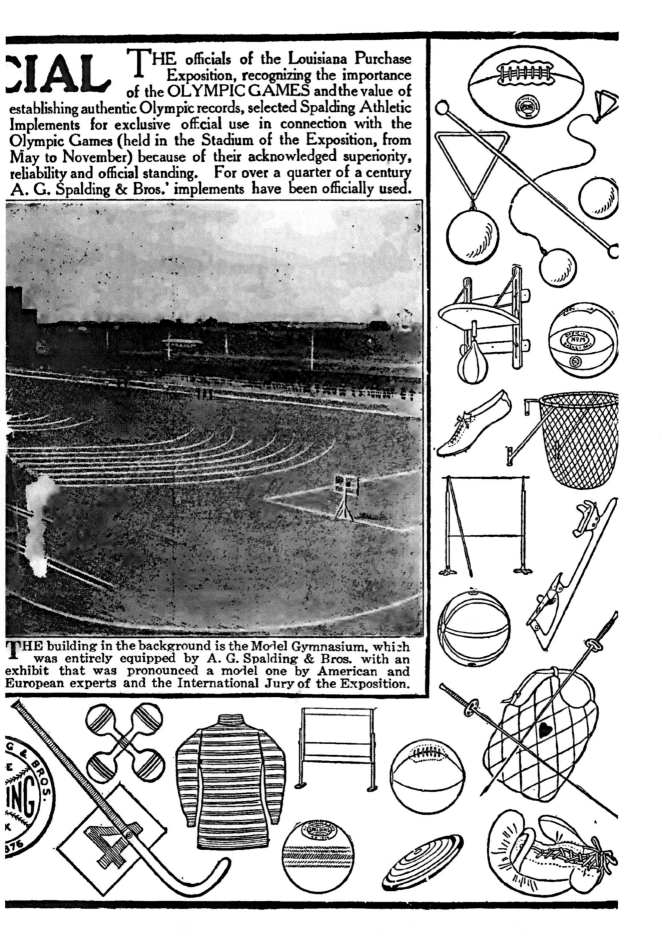

CIAL

THE officials of the Louisiana Purchase Exposition, recognizing the importance of the OLYMPIC GAMES and the value of establishing authentic Olympic records, selected Spalding Athletic Implements for exclusive official use in connection with the Olympic Games (held in the Stadium of the Exposition, from May to November) because of their acknowledged superiority, reliability and official standing. For over a quarter of a century A. G. Spalding & Bros.' implements have been officially used.

THE building in the background is the Model Gymnasium, which was entirely equipped by A. G. Spalding & Bros. with an exhibit that was pronounced a model one by American and European experts and the International Jury of the Exposition.

No. 124—How to Become a Gymnast

By Robert Stoll, of the New York A. C., the American champion on the flying rings from 1885 to 1892. Any boy who frequents a gymnasium can easily follow the illustrations and instructions in this book and with a little practice become proficient on the horizontal and parallel bars, the trapeze or the "horse." Price 10 cents.

No. 128—How to Row

By E. J. Giannini, of the New York A. C., one of America's most famous amateur oarsmen and champions. This book will instruct any one who is a lover of rowing how to become an expert. It is fully illustrated, showing how to hold the oars, the finish of the stroke and other information that will prove valuable to the beginner. Contains also the official laws of boat racing of the National Association of Amateur Oarsmen. Price 10 cents.

No. 129—Water Polo

By Gus Sundstrom, instructor at the New York A. C. It treats of every detail, the individual work of the players, the practice of the team, how to throw the ball, with illustrations and many valuable hints. Price 10 cents.

No. 135 — Official Handbook of the A. A. U. of the United States

The A. A. U. is the governing body of athletes in the United States of America, and all games must be held under its rules, which are exclusively published in this handbook, and a copy should be in the hands of every athlete and every club officer in America. This book contains the official rules for running, jumping, weight throwing, hurdling, pole vaulting, swimming, boxing, wrestling, etc., and is an encyclopedia in itself. Price 10 cents.

No. 136—Official Y. M. C. A. Handbook

Edited by G. T. Hepbron, the well-known athletic authority. It contains the official rules governing all sports under the jurisdiction of the Y. M. C. A., a complete report of the physical directors' conference, official Y. M. C. A. scoring tables, pentathlon rules, many pictures of the leading Y. M. C. A. athletes of the country, official Y. M. C. A. athletic rules, constitution and by-laws of the Athletic League of Y. M. C. A., all around indoor test, volley ball rules; illustrated. Price 10 cents.

No. 138—Official Croquet Guide

Contains directions for playing, diagrams of important strokes, description of grounds, instructions for the beginner, terms used in the game, and the official playing rules. Price 10 cents.

No. 140—Wrestling

Catch as catch can style. By E. H. Hitchcock, M. D., of Cornell, and R. F. Nelligan, of Amherst College. The book contains nearly seventy illustrations of the different holds, photographed especially and so described that anybody who desires to become expert in wrestling can with little effort learn every one. Price 10 cents.

No. 142—Physical Training Simplified

By Prof. E. B. Warman, the well-known physical culture expert. Is a complete, thorough and practical book where the whole man is considered—brain and body. By following the instructions no apparatus is required. The book is adapted for both sexes. The exercises comprise directions as follows: how to stand; how to sit; how to rest; breathing; exercises for the fingers, wrists, elbows, shoulders, neck, hips, knees, ankles; a word about the muscles; the arms and thighs; shoulders and chest; waist; sides; back and abdomen; bowing; bending; twisting; the liver squeezer, etc., étc, Fully illustrated. Price 10 cents.

No. 143 – Indian Clubs and Dumb-Bells

Two of the most popular forms of home or gymnasium exercise. This book is written by America's amateur champion club swinger, J. H. Dougherty. It is clearly illustrated, by which any novice can become an expert. Price 10 cents.

No. 149—The Care of the Body

A book that all who value health should read and follow its instructions. By Prof. E. B. Warman, the well known lecturer and authority on physical culture. The subject is thoroughly treated, as a glance at the following small portion of the contents shows: An all-around athlete; muscular Christianity; eating; diet—various opinions; bill of fare for brain workers; bill of fare for muscle-makers; what to eat and drink; a simple diet; an opinion on brain food; why is food required? drinking water; nutrition—how food nourishes the body; a day's food, how used; constituents of a day's ration—beefsteak, potatoes bread, butter, water; germs of disease; etc. Price 10 cents.

No. 154—Field Hockey

To those in need of vigorous and healthful out-of-doors exercise, this game is recommended highly. Its healthful attributes are manifold and the interest of player and spectator alike is kept active throughout the progress of the game. The game is prominent in the sports at Vassar, Smith, Wellesley, Bryn Mawr and other leading colleges. Price 10 cents.

No. 156—The Athlete's Guide

How to become an athlete. It contains full instructions for the beginner, telling how to sprint, hurdle, jump and throw weights, general hints on training; in fact, this book is one of the most complete on the subject that has ever appeared. Special chapters contain valuable advice to beginners and important A. A. U. rules and their explanations, while the pictures comprise many scenes showing champions in action. Price 10 cents.

No. 157—How to Play Lawn Tennis

A complete description of lawn tennis; a lesson for beginners and directions telling how to make the most important strokes; styles and skill of the experts; the American twist service; how to build and keep a court. Illustrated from photographs of leading players in action. Price 10 cents.

No. 158—Indoor and Outdoor Gymnastic Games

Without question one of the best books of its kind ever published. Compiled by Prof. A. M. Chesley, the well-known Y. M. C. A. physical director. It is a book that will prove valuable to indoor and outdoor gymnasiums, schools, outings and gatherings where there are a number to be amused. The games described comprise a list of 120, divided into several groups. Price 10 cents.

No. 161—Ten Minutes' Exercise for Busy Men

By Dr. Luther Halsey Gulick, superintendent of physical training in the New York public schools. Anyone who is looking for a concise and complete course of physical education at home would do well to procure a copy of this book. Ten minutes' work as directed is exercise anyone can follow. It already has had a large sale and has been highly commended by all who have followed its instructions. Nearly 100 pages of illustrations and 100 of text. Price 10 cents.

No. 162—How to Become a Boxer

For many years books have been issued on the art of boxing, but it has remained for us to arrange a book that we think is sure to fill all demands. It contains over 70 pages of illustrations showing all the latest blows, posed especially for this book under the supervision of one of the best instructors of boxing in the United States, who makes a specialty of teaching and who knows how to impart his knowledge. They are so arranged that anyone can easily become a proficient boxer. The book also contains pictures of all the well known boxers. A partial list of the 200 pages of the book include: A history of boxing; how to box; the correct position; the hands; clenching the fist; the art of gauging distance; the first principles of hitting; the elements of defence; feinting; knockout blows; the chin punch; the blow under the ear; the famous solar plexus knockout; the heart blow; famous blows and their originators: Fitzsimmons' contribution; the McCoy corkscrew; the kidney punch; the liver punch; the science of boxing; proper position of hand and arm; left hook to face; hook to the jaw; how to deliver the solar plexus; correct delivery of a right uppercut; blocking a right swing and sending a right uppercut to chin; blocking a left swing and sending a left uppercut to chin; the side step; hints on training, diet and breathing; how to train; rules for boxing. Price 10 cents.

No. 165—The Art of Fencing

This is a new book by Regis and Louis Senac, of New York, famous instructors and leading authorities on the subject. Messrs. Senac give in detail how every move should be made, and tell it so clearly that anyone can follow the instructions. It is illustrated with sixty full page pictures, posed especially for this book. Price 10 cents.

No. 166—How to Swing Indian Clubs

By Prof. E. B. Warman, the well-known exponent of physical culture. The most complete work on this special subject ever issued. By following the directions carefully anyone can become an expert. Price 10 cents.

No. 167—Quoits

By M. W. Deshong. The need of a book on this interesting game has been felt by many who wished to know the fine points and tricks used by the experts. Mr. Deshong explains them, with illustrations, so that a novice can readily understand. Price 10 cents.

No. 170—Push Ball

Played with an air-inflated ball 6 feet in diameter, weighing about 50 pounds. A side consists of eleven men. This book contains the official rules and a sketch of the game; illustrated. Price 10 cents.

No. 171—Basket Ball for Women

Edited by Miss Senda Berenson, of Smith College. Contains the rules for basket ball for women as adopted by the conference on physical training, held in June, 1899, at Springfield, Mass., and articles on the following subjects: Psychological effects of basket ball for women, by Dr. Luther H. Gulick, superintendent of physical training in the schools of Greater New York; physiological effects of basket ball, by Theodore Hough, Ph. D.; significance of basket ball for women, by Senda Berenson; relative merit of the Y. M. C. A. rules and women's rules, by Augusta Lane Patrick; practical side of basket ball, by Ellen Emerson, B. K., Agnes Childs, A. B., Fanny Garrison. A. B.; A Plea for Basket Ball, by Julie Ellsbee Sullivan, Teachers' College, New York; diagram of field, showing position of team; illustrated with many pictures of basket ball teams. Price 10 cents.

No. 174—Distance and Cross Country Running

By George Orton, the famous University of Pennsylvania runner. Tells how to become proficient at the quarter, half, mile, the longer distances, and cross-country running and steeplechasing, with instructions for training and schedules to be observed when preparing for a contest. Illustrated with numerous pictures of leading athletes in action, with comments by the editor on the good and bad points shown. Price 10 cents.

No. 177—How to Swim

By J. H. Sterrett, the leading authority on swimming in America. The instructions will interest the expert as well as the novice; the illustrations were made from photographs especially posed, showing the swimmer in clear water; a valuable feature is the series of "land drill" exercises for the beginner, which is illustrated by many drawings. The contents comprise: A plea for education in swimming; swimming as an exercise and for development; land drill exercises; plain swimming; best methods of learning; the breast stroke; breathing; under-arm side stroke; scientific strokes-- over-arm side stroke: double over-arm or "trudgeon" stroke; touching and turning; training for racing; ornamental swimming; floating; diving; running header; back dive; diving feet foremost; the propeller; marching on the water; swimming on the back; amateur swimming rules; amateur plunging rules.. Price 10 cents.

No. 178—How to Train for Bicycling

Gives methods of the best riders when training for long or short distance races; hints on training. Revised and up-to-date in every particular. Price 10 cents.

No. 180—Ring Hockey

A new game for the gymnasium, invented by Dr. J. M. Vorhees of Pratt Institute, Brooklyn, that has sprung into instant popularity; as exciting as basket ball. This book contains official rules. Price 10 cents.

No. 182—All-Around Athletics

Gives in full the method of scoring the All-Around Championship, giving percentage tables showing what each man receives for each performance in each of the ten events. It contains as well instructive articles on how to train for the All-Around Championship. Illustrated with many pictures of champions in action and scenes at all-around meets. Price 10 cents.

No. 185—Health Hints

A series of articles by Prof. E. B. Warman, the well known lecturer and authority on physical culture. Prof. Warman treats very interestingly of health influenced by insulation; health influenced by underwear; health influenced by color; exercise, who needs it? Price 10 cents.

No. 187—How to Play Roller Polo

Edited by J. C. Morse. A full description of the game; official rules; pictures of teams; other articles of interest. Price 10 cents.

No. 188—Lawn Hockey, Tether Tennis, Golf Croquet, Volley Ball, Hand Tennis, Garden Hockey, Parlor Hockey, Badminton

Containing the rules for each game. Illustrated. Price 10 cents.

No. 189—Rules for Games

Compiled by Jessie H. Bancroft, director of physical training, department of education, New York City. These games are intended for use at recesses, and all but the team games have been adapted to large classes. Suitable for children from three to eight years, and include a great variety, divided under the general heads of ball games, bean bag games, circle games, singing and miscellaneous games. Price 10 cents.

No. 191—How to Punch the Bag

By W. H. Rothwell ("Young Corbett"), champion featherweight of the world. This book is undoubtedly the best treatise on bag punching that has ever been printed. Every variety of blow used in training is shown and explained. The pictures comprise thirty-three full page reproductions of Young Corbett as he appears while at work in his training quarters. The photographs were taken by our special artist and cannot be seen in any other publication than Spalding's Athletic Library No. 191. Fancy bag punching is treated by a well known theatrical bag puncher, who shows the latest tricks. Price 10 cents.

No. 193—How to Play Basket Ball

By G. T. Hepbron, editor of the Official Basket Ball Guide. Contains full instructions for players, both for the expert and the novice, duties of officials, and specially posed full page pictures showing the correct and incorrect methods of playing. The demand for a book of this character is fully satisfied in this publication, as many points are included which could not be incorporated in the annual publication of the Basket Ball Guide for want of room. Price 10 cents.

No. 194—Racquets, Squash-Racquets and Court Tennis

The need of an authoritative handbook at a popular price on these games is filled by this book. How to play each game is thoroughly explained, and all the difficult strokes shown by special photographs taken especially for this book. Contains the official rules for each game, with photographs of well known courts. Price 10 cents.

No. 195—Official Roque Guide

The official publication of the National Roque Association of America. Edited by Prof. Charles Jacobus, ex-champion. Contains a description of the courts and their construction, diagrams of the field, illustrations, rules and valuable information concerning the game of roque. Price 10 cents.

No. 199—Equestrian Polo Guide

Compiled by H. L. FitzPatrick of the New York Sun. Illustrated with portraits of leading players and contains most useful information for polo players in relation to playing the game, choosing of equipment and mounts; contains the official rules and handicaps of the National Association. Price 10 cents.

No. 200—Dumb-Bells

This is undoubtedly the best work on dumb-bells that has ever been offered. The author, Mr. G. Bojus, of New York City, was formerly superintendent of physical culture in the Elizabeth (N.J.) public schools, instructor at Columbia University, instructor for four years at the Columbia summer school, and is now proprietor of the Liberty Street Gymnasium, at 121 Liberty Street, New York City. The book contains 200 photographs of all the various exercises, with the instructions in large, readable type. It should be in the hands of every teacher and pupil of physical culture, and is invaluable for home exercise as well. Price 10 cents.

No. 201—Lacrosse—From Candidate to Team

By William C. Schmeisser, captain Johns Hopkins University champion intercollegiate lacrosse team of 1902; edited by Ronald T. Abercrombie, ex-captain and coach of Johns Hopkins University lacrosse team, 1900-1904. Every position is thoroughly explained in a most simple and concise manner, rendering it the best manual of the game ever published. Illustrated with numerous snapshots of important plays. Price 10 cents.

No. 202—How to Play Base Ball

Edited by T. H. Murnane. New and revised edition. Contents: How to become a batter, by Napoleon Lajoie, James Collins, Hugh Jennings and Jesse Tannehill; how to run the bases, by Jack Doyle and Frank L. Chance; advice to base runners, by James E. Sullivan, Secretary-Treasurer A.A.U.; how to become a good pitcher, by Cy Young, "Rube" Waddell and Bert Cunningham; on curve pitching, by Cy Young, James J. Callahan, Frank Donahue, Vic Willis, William Dineen and Charley Nichols; how to become a good catcher, by Eddie Phelps, William Sullivan and M. J. Kittridge; how to play first base, by Hugh Jennings; how to play second base, by Napoleon Lajoie and William Gleason; how to play third base, by James Collins and Lave Cross; how to play shortstop, by Herman Long; how to play the infield, by Charles A. Comiskey; how to play the outfield, by Fred Clarke; the earmarks of a ball player, by John J. McGraw; good advice for players; how to organize a team; how to manage a team; how to score a game; how to umpire a game; base ball rules interpreted for boys. Price 10 cents.

No. 204—Official Intercollegiate A.A.A. Handbook

Contains constitution, by-laws, laws of athletics, and rules to govern the awarding of the championship cup of the Intercollegiate Athletic Association of Amateur Athletes of America, the governing body in college athletics. Contains official intercollegiate records from 1876 to 1904, with the winner's name and time in each event, list of points won by each college, and list of officers of the association from 1889 to 1904, inclusive. To anyone interested the book is invaluable as a record. Price 10 cents.

No. 205—Official Handbook of the Public Schools Athletic League

This is the official handbook of the Public Schools Athletic League, which embraces all the public schools of Greater New York. It contains the official rules that govern all the contests of the league, and constitution, by-laws and officers. Edited by Dr. Luther Halsey Gulick, superintendent of physical education in the New York public schools, and Wm. C. J. Kelly, secretary of the league. Illustrated. Price 10 cents.

No. 206—How to Play Golf

No golfer should miss having a copy of this golf guide. Harry Vardon tells how to play game, with life-like illustrations showing the different strokes. The book also contains the revised official rules, official records, as well as pictures of many important players, and a directory giving name, address, membership and length of golf course of clubs in the United States. Price 10 cents.

No. 207–Bowling on the Green; or, Lawn Bowls

How to construct a green; necessary equipment; how to play the game, and the official rules as promulgated by the Scottish Bowling Association. Edited by Mr. James W. Greig. Illustrated. Price 10 cents.

No. 208–Physical Education and Hygiene

This is the fifth of the Physical Training series, by Prof. E. B. Warman (see Nos. 142, 149, 166 and 185), and a glance at the contents will show the variety of subjects: Chapter I—Basic principles; longevity. Chapter II—Hints on eating; food values; the uses of salt. Chapter III—Medicinal value of certain foods. Chapter IV—The efficacy of sugar; sugar, food for muscular work; eating for strength and endurance; fish as brain food; food for the children. Chapter V—Digestibility; bread; appendicitis due to flour. Chapter VI—Hints on drinking—Water, milk, buttermilk, tea, coffee; how to remain young. Chapter VII—Hints on bathing; cold, hot, warm, tepid, salt, sun, air, Russian, Turkish, cabinet. Chapter VIII—Hints on breathing; breathlessness, heart strain, second wind, yawning, the art of yogi. Price 10 cents.

No. 209–How to Become a Skater

Contains advice for beginners; how to become a figure skater thoroughly explained, with many diagrams showing how to do all the different tricks of the best figure skaters, including the Mohawk, with all its variations; Q's, forward and backward, inside and outside; the crosscuts, including the difficult Swedish style; inside and outside spins; the grapevine, with its numerous branches, and many other styles, which will be comparatively simple to any one who follows the directions given. Profusely illustrated with pictures of prominent skaters and numerous diagrams. Price 10 cents.

No. 210–How to Play Foot Ball

Edited by Walter Camp. The contents embrace everything that a beginner wants to know and many points that an expert will be glad to learn. The pictures are made from snapshots of leading teams and individual players in action, with comments by Walter Camp. Price 10 cents.

No. 211–Spalding's Official Foot Ball Guide

Edited by Walter Camp. Contains the new rules, with diagram of field as newly arranged; special chapters on the game, foot ball for the spectator, All-America teams, as selected by leading authorities; Middle West, Southern, Canadian foot ball, records, and pictures of all the prominent teams, embracing nearly 3,000 players. Price 10 cents.

No. 212–Official Basket Ball Guide

Edited by George T. Hepbron. Contains the revised official rules, decisions on disputed points, records of prominent teams, reports on the game from various parts of the country, and pictures of hundreds of players. The standard basket ball annual of the country. Price 10 cents.

No. 213-285 Health Answers

Contents: Necessity for exercise in the summer; three rules for bicycling; when going up-hill; sitting out on summer nights; ventilating a bedroom; ventilating a house; how to obtain pure air; bathing; salt water baths at home; a substitute for ice water; drinking ice water; to cure insomnia; asleep in two minutes; for those who ride wheels; summer outdoor exercise; profuse perspiration; danger of checking perspiration; dress, hot weather, etc., etc. Price 10 cents.

No. 214-Graded Calisthenics and Dumb-Bell Drills

By Albert B. Wegener, Physical Director Y. M. C. A., Rochester, N. Y. Ever since graded apparatus work has been used in gymnastics, the necessity of having a mass drill that would harmonize with it has been felt. For years it has been the established custom in most gymnasiums of memorizing a set drill, never varied from one year's end to the other. Consequently the beginner was given the same kind and amount as the older member. With a view to giving uniformity the present treatise is attempted. Price 10 cents

No. 215-Indoor Base Ball

America's national game is now vieing with other indoor games as a winter pastime. This book contains the playing rules, pictures of leading teams, and interesting articles on the game. Price 10 cents.

No. 216-How to Become a Bowler

By S. Karpf, Secretary of the American Bowling Congress, and one of the best posted men on bowling in America. Contents: History of the sport; diagrams of effective deliveries; how to bowl; a few hints to beginners; American Bowling Congress; the national championships; how to build an alley; how to score; spares—how they are made. Rules for cocked hat, cocked hat and feather, quintet, battle game, nine up and nine down, head pin and four back, ten pins—head pin out, five back, the Newport game, ten pin head pin game, duckpin game, head pin game, Dayton candle (rubber neck) pin game, New England candle pin game. Illustrated with portraits of all the prominent bowlers. Price 10 cents.

No. 217-Official Athletic Almanac

Compiled by J. E. Sullivan, Chief Department Physical Culture, Louisiana Purchase Exposition, and Director Olympic Games, 1904. The only annual publication now issued that contains a complete list of amateur best-on-records; complete intercollegiate records; complete English records from 1866; swimming records; interscholastic records; Irish, Scotch and Australasian records; reports of leading athletic meets; skating records; important athletic events and numerous photos of individual athletes and leading athletic teams. This year's issue is a special Olympic Games number and contains the only full account of the Olympic Games of 1904, and a review of Anthropological Days at the World's Fair stadium, being the first time on record where athletic events were contested in which savages were the exclusive participants, thus forming the first authoritative basis for a comparison between the abilities of the civilized athlete and the savage. Price 10 cents.

No. 218—Ice Hockey and Ice Polo

Written by the most famous player in Canada, A. Farrell, of the Shamrock hockey team of Montreal. It contains a complete description of the game, its origin, points of a good player, and an instructive article on how game is played, with diagrams and official rules. Illustrated with pictures of leading teams. Price 10 cents.

No. 219—Base Ball Percentage Book

To supply a demand for a book which would show the percentage of clubs without recourse to the arduous work of figuring, the publishers of Spalding's Athletic Library have had Mr. John B. Foster, Sporting Editor of the New York Evening Telegram, compile a book which answers every requirement, and which has met with the greatest praise for its accuracy and simplicity. No follower of the game can afford to be without it. Price 10 cents.

No. 220—Official Base Ball Guide

Edited by Henry Chadwick, the "Father of Base Ball," the official publication of base ball. It contains a complete record of all leagues in America, pictures of teams, official rules and reviews of the game. The standard base ball annual of the country. Price 10 cents.

No. 221—Spalding's Lawn Tennis Annual

Contains official statistics, photographs of leading players, special articles on the game, review of important tournaments, official rules, handicapping rules and tables; list of fixtures for the current year and other valuable information. Price 10 cents.

No. 222—Spalding's Official Cricket Guide

Edited by Jerome Flannery. The most complete year book of the game that has ever been published in America. It contains all the records of the previous year, reports of special matches, official rules and pictures of all the leading teams and individual players. Price 10 cents.

An Encyclopedia of Base Ball

Attention is called to the following ten numbers of Spalding's Athletic Library, embracing the greatest collection of books of instruction for playing the various positions in the game that has ever been published. These books are entirely new and up-to-date, and contain the latest methods of play, as only last season's star players were consulted in their compilation. Each number is complete in itself and is profusely illustrated. Be sure and ask for Spalding's Athletic Library. Price 10 cents for each book. For detailed description see following numbers;

No. 223—How to Bat

The most important part of ball playing nowadays, outside of pitching, is batting. The team that can bat and has some good pitchers can win base ball games; therefore, every boy and young man who has, of course, already learned to catch, should turn his attention to this department of the game, and there is no better way of becoming proficient than by reading this book and then constantly practising the little tricks explained therein. It is full of good advice to batsmen, and many good batters will be surprised to find contained in it so many points of which they were unaware. Edited by Jesse F. Matteson of the Chicago American, and profusely illustrated. Price 10 cents.

No. 224—How to Play the Outfield.

Compiled especially for the young player who would become an expert. The best book on playing the outfield that has ever been published. There are just as many tricks to be learned, before a player can be a competent fielder, as there are in any other position on a nine, and this book explains them all. Illustrated with numerous page pictures of leading outfielders. Price 10 cents.

No. 225—How to Play First Base

No other position on a ball team has shown such a change for the better in recent years as first base. Modifications in line with the betterment of the sport in every department have been made at intervals, but in no other department have they been so radical. No boy who plays the initial sack can afford to overlook the points and hints contained in this book. Entirely new and up to date. Illustrated with full page pictures of all the prominent first basemen. Price 10 cents.

No. 226–How to Play Second Base

There are so few men who can cover second base to perfection that their names can easily be called off by anyone who follows the game of base ball. Team owners who possess such players would not part with them for thousands of dollars. These men have been interviewed and their ideas incorporated in this book for the especial benefit of boys who want to know the fine points of play at this point of the diamond. Illustrated with full page pictures. Edited by J. E. Wray, sporting editor Globe-Democrat, St. Louis. Price 10 cents.

No. 227–How to Play Third Base

Third base is, in some respects, the most important of the infield. No major league team has ever won a pennant without a great third baseman. Collins of the Boston Americans and Leach of Pittsburg are two of the greatest third basemen the game has ever seen, and their teams owe much of the credit for pennants they have won to them. These men in this book describe just how they play the position. Everything a player should know is clearly set forth and any boy will surely increase his chances of success by a careful reading of this book. Illustrated. Price 10 cents.

No. 228–How to Play Short-stop

Shortstop is one of the hardest positions on the infield to fill, and quick thought and quick action are necessary for a player who expects to make good as a shortstop. The views of every well known player who covers this position have been sought in compiling this book, and it is offered as being the most complete book of its class ever produced. The boy who would excel at short needs to study it thoroughly. Illustrated. Price 10 cents.

No. 229–How to Catch

Undoubtedly the best book on catching that has yet been published. Every boy who has hopes of being a clever catcher should read how well known players cover their position. Among the more noted ones who describe their methods of play in this book are Lou Criger of the Boston Americans, Johnnie Kling of the Chicago Nationals and Jack O'Connor of the St. Louis Browns. The numerous pictures in the book comprise those of all the noted catchers in the big leagues. Price 10 cents.

No. 230—How to Pitch ·

A new, up-to-date book. Published for the first time this year. No boy can afford to be without a copy of it. Edited by John B. Foster of the Evening Telegram (New York). The object of this book is to aid the beginners who aspire to become clever twirlers, and its contents are the practical teaching of men who have reached the top as pitchers, and who have had experience, both as members of the best clubs playing base ball and as contenders against teams that have enjoyed national reputations. Cy Young, the famous Boston American pitcher, whose steadiness in the box is proverbial, gives advice on control of the ball and tells what a boy should do to obtain it; Sam Leever of the Pittsburgs shows how to pitch the outcurve; William Dineen of the Boston Americans tells how to pitch an inshoot; Thomas Hughes gives hints on pitching the drop; Joe McGinnity, the "iron man," of the New York Nationals, explains how he uses his successful raise ball and his famous "cross fire"; Christy Mathewson, the pride of the New York Polo Grounds, discusses the body swing; Frank Hahn, who is left-handed, has something of interest to those who use that member; John J. McGraw, New York Giants' brilliant manager, discourses on the pitcher as a fielder, and as he started in his base ball career as a twirler, his advice has grounds for attention; Al Orth, the "curveless wonder," tells how to make a batter do what you want him to do; John Powell explains how to act when runners are on bases; Charley Nichols, the former pitcher of the Boston Nationals and now manager of the St. Louis Nationals, describes the jump ball; Frank Sparks treats of change of pace, and Jack Chesbro, the star of the New York Americans' pitching corps, describes at length the "spit" ball, of which he is so famous an exponent. The book is profusely illustrated. Price 10 cents.

No. 231—How to Coach; How to Captain a Team; How to Manage a Team; How to Umpire: How to Organize a League.

A useful guide to all who are interested in the above subjects. Jimmy Collins, manager-captain of the Boston Americans, writes on coaching; M. J. Kelly of the St. Paul champions, on captaining; Al Buckenberger of the Boston Nationals, on managing; Frank Dwyer of the American League staff, on umpiring: Fred Lake on minor leagues, and the editor of the book, T. H. Murnane, President of the New England League, on how to organize a league. Price 10 cents.

No. 232—How to Run the Bases

The importance of base running as a scientific feature of the national game is becoming more and more recognized each year. Besides being spectacular, feats of base stealing nearly always figure in the winning of a game. Many a close contest is decided on the winning of that little strip of 90 feet which lies between cushions. When hits are few and the enemy's pitchers steady, it becomes incumbent on the opposing team to get around the bases in some manner. Effective stealing not only increases the effectiveness of the team by advancing its runners without wasting hits, but it serves to materially disconcert the enemy and frequently has caused an entire opposing club to temporarily lose its poise and throw away the game. This book gives clear and concise directions for excelling as a base runner; tells when to run and when not to do so; how and when to slide; team work on the bases; in fact, every point of the game is thoroughly explained. In addition such clever men as Harry Bay, the fleet footed Clevelander; Frank Chance, Bill Dahlen and Hans Wagner describe their methods of action. Illustrated with pictures of leading players. Price 10 cents.

No. 233—Jiu Jitsu

A complete description of this famous Japanese system of self-defence. Each move thoroughly explained and illustrated with numerous full page pictures of Messrs. A. Minami and K. Koyama, two of the most famous exponents of the Jiu Jitsu in America, who posed especially for this book. Be sure and ask for the Spalding Athletic Library book on Jiu Jitsu. Price 10 cents.

Spalding's Athletic Library is for sale by all department stores, athletic and sporting goods dealers and newsdealers.

SPALDING'S HOME LIBRARY

Devoted to Games and Amusements for the Home Circle

1—Chess	16—Piquet
2—Whist	17—Go-Bang
3—Dominoes and Dice	18—Games of Patience
4—Poker	19—Children's Games
5—Backgammon	20—Cribbage
6—Euchre	21—Drawing Room Games
7—Billiards	22—Group of Card Games
8—Ecarte	23—Children's Games
9—Checkers	24—Group of Card Games
10—Bezique	25—Drawing Room Games
11—Pool	26—Group of Card Games
12—Pinochle	27—Children's Games
13—Lotto	28—Skat
14—Hearts	29—Drawing Room Games
15—Reversi	30—Baccarat

PRICE 10 CENTS PER COPY

CPSIA information can be obtained at www.ICGtesting.com
Printed in the USA
LVOW051700281111

256813LV00004B/144/P